LIVES OF THE DEAD

Lives of the Dead
COLLECTED POEMS of Hanoch Levin

Translated by Atar Hadari
with an introduction by Igal Sarna

Arc
PUBLICATIONS
2018

Published by Arc Publications,
Nanholme Mill, Shaw Wood Road
Todmorden OL14 6DA, UK
www.arcpublications.co.uk

978 1908376 64 0 (pbk)
978 1908376 65 7 (hbk)
978 1908376 66 4 (ebk)

ACKNOWLEDGEMENTS

The translation of the long poem 'Lives of the Dead' first
appeared in *Poetry* magazine in May, 2009. The publishers
are grateful to Lilian Bareto for granting permission to
reproduce the text of the poems in the original Hebrew, and
for the translation rights. Thanks are due to Igal Sarna for
allowing an edited version of his article in *Yediot Aharonot*
to be translated and reproduced by way of an introduction
to this book. The publishers and the translator are grateful
to Jessica Cohen for her help with facilitating this project.

Design by Tony Ward
Printed in Great Britain by T.J. International Ltd,
Padstow, Cornwall

Cover picture: Marcus Ward

This book has been selected to receive financial assistance from
English PEN's 'PEN Translates' programme, supported by Arts
Council England. PEN exists to promote literature and our
understanding of it, to uphold writers' freedoms around the
world, to campaign against the persecution and imprisonment of
writers for stating their views, and to promote the friendly
co-operation of writers and the free exchange of ideas.

ENGLISH PEN — FREEDOM TO WRITE, FREEDOM TO READ

LOTTERY FUNDED | ARTS COUNCIL ENGLAND — Supported using public funding by

Arc Publications Translations series
Series Editor: Jean Boase-Beier

CONTENTS

For Baruch Joel Shlomo

in whose pram basket the book of poems lay
to translate while he napped

In the car to my father's funeral, my uncle (who had never cared for my father) told me that I really should translate this book of poems called *Lives of the Dead*. He's not a man who reads poetry but he'd read this book and had liked it, as had many people: it had gone through several editions in Israel. The following year I translated *Ecclesiastes* as a way of dealing with my father's passing, and it is as sober a meditation on death as I can imagine. I then came across *Lives of the Dead* again, having avoided it despite my uncle's suggestion. A year later, the humour of the book, and particularly the long title poem, spoke to me rather more than in the year of mourning, and the tone of delicacy, scatological cruelty, and wistful sadness attracted me. I took *Ecclesiastes* to be a poem trying hard to find a meaning in life, all but failing, and only finally turning to the necessity of faith in God. In Hanoch Levin's poems, especially in *Lives of the Dead*, I found a profane, rude, unavoidably direct and modern answer to *Ecclesiastes* – a look at death by someone who very much did not believe in the "afterlife" but nevertheless saw and expressed all the hopes which even the most irreligious keep in the deepest, most secret closets of their heart: *What, didn't you know that after death there is a summer camp and God is the lifeguard?*

Levin's response to the terminal illness which led to his premature death was this book of mordant, witty, and unflinching poems on the subject. A mixture of philosophy, erotic jealousy about his surviving lover, and sheer funniness about the horrific prospect at hand, the book is unusually concentrated for a collection of poems. Most collections are composed here and there, and bring together the work of some years which may have a common theme but does not, usually, respond to one large truth bearing down on the author with the directness of a freight train. In this case one never fails to hear the whistle howling at the poet's back.

Problems. It does rhyme, so the English in my view had to rhyme. But Hebrew is a much more compact language than English, so a real difficulty was making the much longer sets of beats in English keep moving to sustain the line unit and rhyme scheme. This is the sixth draft, and the changes were mostly to improve rhyme and eliminate syllables. Another problem was the tone, which required a slang of a particular place and a choice between America and England. I opted for England, while being aware that every English colloquialism has to balance its gain in tone against the risk of lost clarity to a potential reader. But I finally situated the poem firmly in the waves at the heart of the Atlantic, because Hebrew, among many idiosyncrasies, has a Bible-sourced tic of reiterating an action by using a verb and noun of the same root, as in "cried his cry." In English that meant that "nappied with nappies" had to make way for the American "diapered with diapers," for the sake of accepted usage. The tone in Hebrew weaves skilfully from low to high but is never obscure, so clarity and speed were, as in any epic, the essence of the enterprise.

Though he began as a poet, Levin made his name as a playwright, satirist and popular lyricist: he is the most performed playwright of the Israeli stage. A comparison with Brecht is in fact not misleading. The long poem 'Lives of the Dead' is his last comic turn and tragic aria.

I do not know if there is a heaven offering judgement, or merely a graveyard full of laughing skulls, as Levin expected – perhaps he is in one of those places now, viewing his readers; perhaps he is laughing still, the way that the reader of this last of his works often will – laughing open mouthed like a skull, spread-jawed in horror. He was no respecter of form and gave no interviews – he wanted things to speak for themselves. So nothing much has changed, except that this particular production did not have the benefit of his quiet direction on its way to the auditorium.

Atar Hadari

INTRODUCTION: THE NATIONAL POET'S MOTHER

The following is an abridged version of the writer Igal Sarna's 6000-word feature story on Hanoch Levin, written for the Israeli daily newspaper Yediot Aharonot.

Hanoch Levin spies on the neighbourhood, I spy on Levin. Like the long line, one after the other, in the story *Frustration*, where Levin wrote: "The life of a Peeping Tom is difficult and full of wear and tear." Since I was a boy I've seen many of his shows. Always, afterwards, I felt tremendous relief as if after prolonged observation through military night vision binoculars, or a powerful telescope. I didn't know a thing about him but the Polish stratagems of his protagonists had a familiar tone due to the shared provenance of our ancestors.

In the recesses of my brain lurked a report that Levin's origins and childhood were in a South Tel Aviv neighbourhood. He himself refused to talk. There was no surprise in that. What was more surprising was the silence of his friends, even those he'd not seen for many years. Friends from high school were well acquainted, even fifteen years after, with his introversion. When I approached them, they sought his consent. Levin preferred them not to speak with me. The available material on him in theatre archives is scant and provides, for the most part, inaccurate biographical details. Of his religious education he spoke only once: at a personal audience with the President of Israel, Ephraim Katzir. There he said a few sentences about Yaavetz High School. A friend remembered his mother's house sketchily as "a corner building near the central bus station". I scoured the staircases of corner buildings, all black and dingy with shattered mail boxes and ancient external protective walls. In the abandoned buildings used heroin syringes from the night before rolled on the floor; inside I also found Malka Levin, who spoke to me through the crack of the door. I was holding onto the door handle, she was pulling from the other side. At the end of the street stood the synagogue described minutely in the poetic sequence *Morning Prayers*, an ancient commemorative, laden with inscriptions to memorialize the dead, a sort of collective memory of the neighbourhood.

I watched him receive the Israel Prize in the sky blue Recanati Auditorium, spying on the crowd of critics, emerging for a moment from the offices at the Tzavta arts centre, passing with a loaf of still warm bread on Dizengoff. In the city archive on Bialik, I leafed through old housing development plans and the Tel Aviv chronic condition. I saw the panic of Feuterstein at the Observer reappear fourteen years later in Taasa Glazer, the Yemenite. Now I know a few biographical details about Hanoch Levin and a few about the country he saw about him from his peculiar viewpoint. But I've no reason to run and bruit it about: I've understood, like the old functionary who comes out of the operating room after the death of Kaspar Hauser[1], and think that a tiny distortion they found in Hauser's brain explains all the wondrous phenomenon of the dead man. Frustration lies in wait here for anyone seeking a simple solution for something that has a million connections.

Levin is very famous, photographed against his will, recipient of the Israel Prize, [Israel's Nobel], and people go to all his shows—but you know nothing about him. In the exhibitionist Israeli reality, which leaves no detail to the imagination, this is an unprecedented phenomenon, this concealment, spying from the darkness, a one-man underground, emerging from time to time to strike and disappear again from sight. The fear of exposure hovers over him like the fear of death. The solution lies, perhaps, in a story called *The National Poet*, who has an entire class sitting in his room, against his will, peeping at his writing, and then stoning him to death.

Over ten years ago Uri Raf wrote about Levin's creations, who make their way from the Florentine neighbourhood in downwardly mobile South Tel Aviv to the Herzlia suburbs, leaving a path of destruction, of crushed souls and depleted values. Levin followed his protagonists. He lives today in

---

[1] Kaspar Hauser was a German youth who claimed to have grown up in the total isolation of a darkened cell. Hauser's claims, and his subsequent death by stabbing, sparked much debate and controversy.

the Herzlia suburbs, in an unpretentious block of flats in a forgettable shopping centre. Levin lives there with his second wife, Edna, an El Al stewardess, and his two small boys.

After the initial great hit of *Hefetz* in 1972, when reviewers recited the complete Hallell of high holidays over young Levin, the reviewer of *Hatzofe*, Dr. Emile Feurstein, a sworn antagonist of Levin, wrote: "It appears to us that this humbug about his curious types and his ridiculous plot is not worthy of being called a play. It's just the chatter of a youngster who passionately detests everyone around him… There's no trace of local colour. This plot could occur in Honolulu." Mr. Feurstein, raging more than any other critic, spoke of Honolulu, but he knew, in his secret heart of shocked hearts, that he himself was standing at the focal point of disturbance: European Jewish, faithful to the tradition, with the shadow of the Holocaust over his head.

Hanoch Levin was born in a house on Rosh Pina street at the corner of Akiva Eiger. On the bus that leaves the central bus station you've passed it hundreds of times: the crumbling cornices, blinds shuttered against the street just a metre away from the stinking exhaust of the buses. The graffiti on the wall: "Stop Stealing Organs from the Dead." If there happened to be an opened window you could peep in at the dark scene, like a studio stage setting, of poor furnishings and bare lighting in a place where the Polish bourgeoisie set its foot fifty years ago and starved to death.

His parents, Malka and Israel Levin, came from Lodz. When they migrated to Tel Aviv in 1935 they brought a nine month old son David with them, who'd been born in Lodz, and left behind their families, parents, brothers and sisters. This was the fifth migration, a last large burst of Jews from Germany, America and Eastern Europe, who arrived with large fortunes and tiny fortunes, and Bialik wrote: "We're proud of the pride and bloom of a place where there's nothing but the empty din of profiteering." It was no longer the time of pioneers. Whoever came was looking for a house, a shop, a kiosk, they thought of getting established, a little respect, economic security, a livelihood. They ran into the Levant and were hardly impressed. They sometimes reminisced about those family evenings over there in Europe and whinged: Tel Aviv, a small town that grew quickly, providing housing for a deposit and an exhausting struggle for livelihood. Malka's brother and sister migrated too. Contact with the home in Lodz was maintained. The parents, the brother and sister stayed there.

Hanoch was born in December 1943. A bad year for a baby. Unfortunate timing. His parents knew that in the Lodz ghetto they were dying of starvation and plagues. In the chilly winter of Tel Aviv in the Neve Sha'anan neighbourhood where the family rented a three-bedroom flat on the corner of Rosh Pina, there was circumcision for the baby; in Europe snow was falling on the deceased. David, aged nine, looked at the newcomer now joining the long-standing family trio. The parents Malka and Israel were no longer a young couple – around 37 years old. They wondered how to fill a new mouth. The baby crying in his basket took in the smell of onion, the hard-boiled egg, and the whisper of anxiety and unease: signs of life among "survivors" busy with eating, mating and livelihood while their families perished in Europe. Later things became clear, the names of the dead and manner of their death became known. The neighbourhood, seized up with shock and bereavement, kept on busying itself with eating, livelihood, mating. They didn't sit mourning for seven days, there was no relief from the ceremonies of bereavement, the bodies of the loved ones were not brought to earth, the place of their death was unknown. Their ashes floated and rested over everything. Mourning became a part of life. The faraway death forbade every pleasure, forged a sense of guilt that Levin later defined: "His mouth is full of sand, my mouth is full of suet." In the summer of '45, when the baby Hanoch was crawling on the floor, it was announced that Hitler was dead. A new threat hovered in the air – the struggle with the Arabs heated up. The Jewish underground movements struck the British but the call-up never reached the neighbourhood. People stayed detached from the heroism, the putter-up of anti-British posters or blower-up of bridges. They got up early to bring the milk into the grocery. In the tiny synagogue at the end of Eiger Street tiny candles burned in memory of the relations of Mr. Aaron Kosman who were slaughtered, suffocated and burned by the Nazis and their helpers, may their names be erased. The British left and the great war broke out. On Saturday morning a siren was heard and in the corridor of the Levin family, on the ground floor, the neighbours and their children gathered. Egyptian planes were dropping bombs on the central bus station a few hundred metres away, and the thunder shook the flat. Hanoch, six years old, wrote in childish print his first poem. Since then he never stopped.

The schoolboy Hanoch Levin, with his little yarmulke, crossed two streets, narrow or lined with traffic, to Neve Shaanan 17, the Religious State School Yaavetz, run by the Mizrachi Workers party. If you seek it today, over a shoe shop, you won't find it. The headmaster, Yehuda Mergel, closed it in 1967. Now Mergel the pensioner remembers Hanoch, "An introverted child, who sat in the corner in absolute silence and looked at the teacher, different from the neighbourhood Swiss natives." Mergel gets emotional: "They had, those Levin boys, some kind of nobility" – when Hanoch came to Year 1 his brother was already in high school, outside the neighbourhood. The next image carved in the memory of the aged headmaster is of the crisis the Levin boy underwent, a shock observed by the experienced educator. Hanoch was already twelve-and-a-half years old, and Israel Levin, the father, not yet fifty, died of a heart attack one morning at the end of winter 1956; when he wanted to get up, as usual, before dawn, his hands and feet would not obey him, Malka Levin approached his bed, the neighbour came in, the boy Hanoch stood and watched the doctor pronounce the hour of his death. The breadwinner father who'd done his best but hadn't succeeded in freeing his family from the deteriorating neighbourhood that anybody who could do so got up and fled.

Meir in the old grocery across from the synagogue has his

own definition of Israel Levin's death: "He went home, Levin, a grocer exactly the same as me, he had a grocery store in town, he had enough troubles of his own, of course he didn't make it, I knew him very well and we talked plenty of times." Meir stands now outside his own grocery which offers almost nothing apart from a few plastic containers of milk and cream cheese. Whoever saw him on Levin's stage would jump from his seat and shout: "That's it: a cruel caricature entirely lacking in local colour." Fifty years now he's been in this store, which is in Neve Shaanan and not Honolulu. This is where Israel Levin sometimes stopped to talk a little about his troubles. On Meir's scalp perches a cap, the nose is ruddy with blood vessels burst from too many years of sunshine, drenched in thick Vaseline for protection, in his ears cotton wool is stuffed, the shoes have open toes and grey socks peep out. As Meir speaks I actually consider Levin's artistic restraint and those who accused him of exaggeration and distortion. "This is where I've been buried alive since 1932, Galician Pole, I live with an ulcer, with a wound, and can't talk, but I talk, who am I, poor thing, what do I get for it, bupkis. I'm sick of it, there are days I work and I cry, what did I need it all for, I wanted to leave Israel in '33 for America, schmamerika, Australia, Switzerland. What did we come here for, to die like dogs. It's all hatred and filth this city, each one hating the other, disgusting. A Jew without money ain't got no life." In his pocket the father kept poems by Hanoch – in his grey "survivor" life that hasn't many pleasures left in it...

Hanoch was then filling up exercise books with poems about orphanhood and the neighbourhood and the wars in the world. In due course he would hand a thick packet to Menachem Perry, editor of *Bookmark*. The poems of a highly sensitive orphaned youth with an astonishingly acute ear for the Polish expressions heard, affecting a stylistic adaptation of pain into a language quite cleansed of emotion. All that was Levinesque was already there in the early poems. Lines such as "Chasing bum after bum, what'll be the final sum?" which Perry quotes to me by heart. An outburst of talent, he says, an outburst rather than a slow development. "He laid his hand on the chilled brow of his father and allowed the orphan's tears that lack all happiness to flow. But his groans emerged like limericks and the honking of his nose sounded like a refrain." (Hanoch Levin, "Spur", *The Back Page*, December 1965.) Or like the Kierkegaardian aphorism – "What is a poet? A miserable man in whose heart a great dread wails but whose lips are formed so that the groans and cries that traverse them turn to enchanting music."

And after the funeral they went back home, a boy at the beginning of adolescence and a mother aged 50. Dad left no money, David was studying theatre in London. The profound grief over his father joined the ancient ache, the personal insecurity got mixed up in the new war at the end of '56. The euphoria of the third kingdom of Israel – and immediately the fall to a panicked retreat in the wake of threats from a distant superpower. Hanoch sat and wrote – orphan-hood got mixed up with the war and with staying put, now just he and his mother. "It was very hard, the pain was great, but whoever lives – lives, there's no monkey business and a man is just a man, there's nothing to be done." (*The Back Page*, 29.11.65)

"Father died exactly twenty-seven-and-a-half years ago," Levin's mother tells me. She spies at me through the narrow crack between the door and the jamb, more than that she won't open. Still in the same old flat, on the corner of Rosh Pina street. The black graffiti is still on the walls: "Stop Stealing Organs from the Dead". An external wall is also still there from some old war.

Hanoch finished primary school at Yaavetz and went to Zeitlin, City High School B for Boys which was attached to the City High School C for Girls, but with the segregation emphasized. There they insisted on matching uniforms and sky blue yarmulke. At the parents' evening, Gottlieb the literature teacher told Malka Levin about her son Hanoch: "he'll be a writer, that there's no arguing about – but not a religious man." The writing reflected scepticism, not fear of heaven. Zeitlin, a religious and exclusive school, prided itself on the quality of its staff and produced year after year of excellent students, many of whom chose the secular path. The satirist B. Michael went there too, he says, "Some of the students are still not shot of the sexual hang-ups from the sexual segregation they imposed there. Their anal sexual fixations were formed there, the crazed urge of adolescent boys for sex and, along with that, the disgust and repression." Rabbi Meir Shapira would give sermons in class on lust, "Think to yourself what they do over there," he would shout, "Why, it's disgusting." Hanoch Levin does not appear on the graduate roll. The tuition fees were a heavy burden, Malka Levin didn't want to go asking for help, and Hanoch, who wore a yarmulke only when eating, transferred for his mother's sake, and maybe even happily, to City High School A evening classes, the first time free classes were instituted.

Here he did not escape the eye of the literature instructor, Ezra Gross, an ancient teacher with not long to go before his pension, a short and emaciated man. To Malka Levin he promised that her son would be an author and in the staff room he was a passionate advocate of the student Levin when the mathematics teacher expressed some reservations. In class Gross's face was on fire when he opened the pages of *Les Fleurs du Mal* to read a poem. His leg rested on the teacher's chair and from the trouser leg the end of his long underwear peeped out, but the students were swept up by his reading: "And it came to pass that the poet, like a heavenly decree, appeared in this world full of rage – his mother was thrown into panic and clenched her fists in rage at the Lord on high." When Levin published his first works and the touchingly sensitive satire, nationalism frothed against him and his mother walked with her head towards the ground. But success and fame, as is their wont, softened the shame. The headmaster Joshua Hager remembers Levin's eyes. "A boy in cheap clothes."

In the last year of school they knuckled down to prepare for their exams. In 1961 the 10th graduating class of City High School A evening classes were photographed and went their separate ways into the army. Hanoch was now outside the neighbourhood as a trainee on the military technology course and for the first time could look back on the old quarter, on the "survivors", on the Poles who got stuck in the darkened streets with their lost self-respect.

In 1979, at an evening dedicated to Hanoch on the Tel Aviv campus, lecturer Dr. Shlomit Vardinon noted that in that very auditorium in the Gilman Building, the student Levin had sat and studied literature at the feet of poet and lecturer Natan Zach. On the basis of his essays as a student he deserved, she said, a professorial chair. Here too his talents did not escape alert eyes. And Zach published the student Levin's sequence *Morning Prayers*, writing about it that Levin had done for a Tel Aviv neighbourhood what Dylan Thomas had done for a Welsh village in *Under Milk Wood*. But it was not the poetry sequence which made Levin's name. What made his name initially was actually his satirical column in the student journal *Spur*. The campus was then ruled by left-wingers. The student paper was managed by Amnon Zaban, Avi Oz, Dudu Halevi and others. The editorial board gave Hanoch the "back page" for satire, to stir the sleepy student body from its slumbers. Levin did not disappoint. In the columns he published from 1965-1967 under the title "Back Page" you may find familiar Levinesque content along with added extras which disappeared with time. Levin also wrote soldier songs, notices regarding grand opening of the public latrine "Defecation Hill", and a small advertisement calling on Arab youth to step up to the challenges awaiting them in the sanitation department of the municipality of Tel Aviv. When the November edition of *Spur* appeared with this ad in it, approximately four hundred enraged students signed a petition protesting the "affront against sensibilities", the "cheap attitude" and so forth. The last signatory on the petition was Hanoch Levin: "Thank you all, that's just what I was getting at." It was the first public response to Levin's work and from that time on it would be an inseparable element of the curious and almost sado-masochistic relationship between Levin and his audience. At university Hanoch Levin got to know the gang from *Vayaktiv*. Menachem Binzki had poetry evenings at his home where Moti Barhav, Amnon Zaban, Michael Drucks and Danny Tratch would meet. Levin, detached from actual political activity, took no part in planning demonstrations but responded to political topics such as Israeli Arabs or relations with Germany which were then simmering on campus, but in his own style. Zaban, who knew Levin, was astonished at the way this tough content was emerging from this silent and self-effacing man. Even then the dichotomy, or even the conflict, between the gentle man and the crude content, was apparent. This was, according to Amnon Zaban, "the true beginning of real Israeli satire that dealt directly with political questions and with the Jewish soul."

Levin's language was a new Hebrew with words sharp as shivs. Clean writing without any sentimentality. Levin studied, worked in the box office of the theatre club, collaborated on pieces with the painter Michael Drucks and got very friendly with Danny Tratch, the draughtsman. A strong bond was also formed at that time with Vitek Tratch, Danny's brother, and in due course they made the film *Fantasy on a Romantic Theme*. When the dam broke and Levin's works were published, things started coming to the surface with some force. A poem in *Haaretz*, powerful prose fragments accompanied by drawings or montages by Drucks, a poem about the singer Audrey Mispreim in the avant-garde journal *Gog* edited by Meir Wieseltier. It took until 1967 for Levin's satirical drama to burst out and strike for the first time. The Six Day War and a crude wave of nationalism made it abundantly clear that the old neighbourhood with all its Polish pride, self-righteousness and its mutual humiliations, had burst its geographical bounds. Levin's telescopic eye detected the shallow depths of the national soul with the diagnosis he'd brought from home. In January 1968 a first draft of *General War Due to End of Supply* was completed – a satirical cabaret bill with songs by Menachem Binzki. The draft stayed in the drawer. What was produced in August 1968 was called: *You, Me and the Next War*. On the stage of the "Barbarians" theatre club the actors declaimed: "And the Private shall live with the Sergeant Major, and the Sergeant Major shall lie with the General, and a small boy shall cover the bodies." They told the viewers before the show: "In an effort to counter-balance the multi-coloured triumphalist carnival…". Levin wanted to hit, not to counter-balance. The tools were already in his hands. Now the viewers filled the darkened studio of "Barbarians" and watched the stage, Levin sat in the wings and spied on the crowd. On the stage he rages, deals in emissions, in farts, in Daddy's constipation, in humiliation and disrespect. Of T. S. Eliot it was once written that he was "a bashful exhibitionist who didn't have the strength to reveal himself all the way, but also refused, to the same extent, to remain locked and sealed to everything outside." The extreme polarisation of the artist's soul: an exhibitionist Peeping Tom like Verdale's father who preferred to spy on life so as not to get hurt. Everything burst out in the shows, everything they didn't talk about in the neighbourhood bubbled up there from under the thin surface. All that the boy had felt and known it was forbidden to mention. The pain became a powerful engine. Levin, a creative artist with backward propulsion, driven by fear and bitterness and hatred. "If Eli Wiesel is the author of the Holocaust and the dead, then Hanoch Levin is the poet of the survivors." He wanted to tell the audience, "Take off the masks, see how you really look." But the audience disappointed him, at the shows they laughed. "It saddens me," he once said, "my entire purpose it not to cause them pleasure but to beat them until it comes out of their ears." Only when he kicked them in the nationalist balls did they scream in rage, kick back, and stop the production. If he was looking for panic, hatred and violent responses he found them in political satire. *You, Me and the Next War* was swiftly closed. They shouted at him, "Whacko, crazy man, communist."

When he rummaged in the twisted soul of the neighbourhood that had already spread over the whole of Israel, they applauded enthusiastically but when he portrayed the same fraudulent Polish stratagems when they starred on the stage of national politics, the audience stormed the stage.

And in a survey of students, a third year law student called Amnon Dankner (later the editor of Israel's largest daily paper), said that he actually opposed the opinions presented in the cabaret fiercely, but objected to the vandals disrupting the event even more. Arieh Goldblum published a paid ad in *Haaretz* in which he called upon anyone who enjoyed the show to rise to the occasion and destroy the state. Responses to *The Queen of the Bathtub*, Levin's third satire, were so extreme that the Cameri Theatre swiftly closed the show. When the suggestion was floated of reviving the show in some cellar, some of the actors announced they would not take part in the underground production for fear of the audience. Even Levin's reserve duty schedule was altered for reasons he attributed to minister of Defense Moshe Dayan and his viewing of *The Queen of the Bathtub*. Levin did not go underground: in the fifteen years since 1968 he has produced eighteen plays, filled auditoria from Eilat to Metula and earned a powerful lobby of admiring critics.

As I sit at one end of Dizzengof with Menachem Perry, Hanoch Levin goes by with a warm loaf of bread. He stops to greet Perry, and goes on his way. Perry testifies that he's a very honest man with outstanding principles for present day Israel and entirely lacking in the egotistical issues that prevail in the artistic community here. Razia Cohen, who played The Great Whore of Babylon, tells me how precise Levin's direction is and the pleasure she took in working with him. "A man with a lovely scent of soap" who gives actors, animals and children nicknames just like he does the characters on his stage. "The nickname is always an accurate and succinct definition of some central quality of that person and with a Yiddish twang." Razia searches for some analogy or metaphor for what she feels like when Levin the director is sitting in the aisle. Finally she says: "It's like somebody's wandering about the house while you're playing piano, and even if he isn't listening, it gives you a warm sense of security."

Albert Cohen, a few minutes before *Rubber Merchants*, remembered his first meeting with Levin when he first came to the Cameri to direct one of his plays. It was *Yaakovi and Leidenthal* and Levin, embarrassed, told Zahrira Harifai and Albert Cohen: "You're very old hands and I'm green, how about you help me out."

After twelve years of working closely with Levin, Albert Cohen says that Levin is "clear of any Levinesqueness, a great and true patriot who responds to everything with his own macabre humour and won't ever leave here even when everybody else has already fled." Only Levin remains free of the Levinesque, his friends will tell you. He doesn't hate women, he loves women and is a family man living in Herzlia with his wife and children and worries about his mother who stayed behind in the neighbourhood. Another youthful friend notes, in a curious line of defence, that he's "a Labour Party man in his political views", as if that would make him more human and comprehensible. Thus two Levins exist side by side: the man, with the smell of farts and onions, on stage, and this one, in the last row, with the good smell of soap. The more the fame of the one grows, the more the other one disappears, refusing to be interviewed, evading prizes. Even these words written here have evinced no response from him but I've been told: expect an answer at a later date. Maybe some story or play will appear with a journalist spying through a keyhole at somebody on the other side who is spying on him.

Igal Sarna, translated by Atar Hadari

MORNING PRAYERS
ברכות השחר

שִׁירוּ לַאֲדֹנָי שִׁיר חָדָשׁ.

כָּךְ כָּךְ, מַר שֶׁרְשֶׁבְסְקִי,
כְּשֶׁבִּקַּשְׁתָּ לָקוּם, כְּדַרְכְּךָ, לִפְנֵי עֲלוֹת הַשַּׁחַר,
לֹא נִשְׁמְעוּ לְךָ יָדֶיךָ,
לֹא נִשְׁמְעוּ לְךָ רַגְלֶיךָ.
הַגֶּשֶׁם יָרַד וְיָרַד עַל בֵּית-הַכְּנֶסֶת
וְאוֹר הַחַשְׁמַל כְּבָר הֵאִיר וְנָדַף רֵיחַ הַבְּצָל.
אָז נִגְּשָׁה אֵלֶיךָ אִשְׁתְּךָ,
אָז נִכְנְסָה הַשְּׁכִינָה בְּבֶהָלַת שְׁכֵנִים,
אָז בָּא גַם הָרוֹפֵא וְקָבַע אֶת מוֹתְךָ
וּפִיו רַעֲנָן מִמִּשְׁחַת שִׁנַּיִם.
הַגֶּשֶׁם יָרַד וְיָרַד עַל בֵּית-הַכְּנֶסֶת.
בַּמִּנְיָן הָרִאשׁוֹן תָּמְהוּ מֶה הָיָה לְךָ,
בַּמִּנְיָן הַשֵּׁנִי כְּבָר יָדְעוּ הַכֹּל,
וּבְבִרְכַּת כֹּהֲנִים יָרְדָה שְׁכִינָה צְרוּדָה
בִּגְרוֹנוֹ שֶׁל הַכֹּהֵן.

כָּךְ, מַר שֶׁרְשֶׁבְסְקִי,
מַתָּ בְּטֶרֶם יוֹם,
בֵּין ג' בְּאִיָּר לְבֵין ד' בְּאִיָּר,
נִשָּׂא בֵּין שׁוֹשְׁבִינֵי הַזְּמָן
אֶל חֻפַּת הָאֲדָמָה.
כָּךְ, מַר שֶׁרְשֶׁבְסְקִי,
בְּטֶרֶם הַיּוֹם הֵאִיר
וּגְרוֹנְךָ מָלֵא בֵּאלֹהִים נוֹרָא
חָבַרְתָּ אֶל הַתַּרְנְגוֹלִים בְּצַוְחָה אֲרֻכָּה;
רַבִּי מֵאִיר בַּעַל הַנֵּס קוֹרֵא מִקֻּפְּסַת פַּח רֵיקָה.

Sing to the Lord a New Song

Just like that, Mr. Shrevrevsky
when you wanted to get up as usual, before dawn,
your hands would not obey,
your feet would not obey.
The rain fell and fell on the synagogue
and an electric light was already burning
and the smell of onion was wafting.
Then your wife leaned across,
then the neighbour came in in a fright the way a neighbour does,
then the doctor came and certified the hour of your death
with his breath all toothpaste minty fresh.
The rain fell and fell on the synagogue.
At the first service they wondered where you went,
at the second service they already knew
and at the Priests' blessing a hoarse Divine Presence
entered the throat of the Priest.

Just like that, Mr. Shrevrevsky,
dead before day began,
between the 3rd and 4th of June
carried away by the ushers of time
to the wedding canopy of the ground.

Just like that, Mr. Shrevresvsky, before day light
with your throat quite full of a terrible God
you joined cocks in a long flight:
Rabbi Meir master of miracles cries from an empty tin can.

הַשֶּׁמֶשׁ, מַר זִילְבֶּרְשְׁטֵיְין, נָעַל אֶת הַתֵּיבָה.
רוּחַ קָרָה שֶׁעָבְרָה מְשַׂחֶקֶת בִּטְנִיס וְאוֹבַּנֵּי יְלָדִים
חָדְרָה בְּעַד סִדְקֵי הַחַלּוֹן
וְנִפְנְפָה אֶת שָׂרָה בֵּילָה בַּת מָרְתָא
הָרְקוּמָה עַל הַפָּרֹכֶת לְזֵכֶר עוֹלָם,
נִפְנְפָה אוֹתָהּ וְנִפְנְפָה אוֹתָהּ לְזֵכֶר עוֹלָם.
תנצב"ה.

מַר זִילְבֶּרְשְׁטֵיְין כִּבָּה אֶת הָאוֹר
שֶׁעַל עַמּוּד שְׁלִיחַ-צִבּוּר.
לַיְלָה יָרַד עַל נִדְבַת רָפָאֵל בֶּטֶר
לְזֵכֶר בְּנוֹ הַחַיָּל מֹשֶׁה
שֶׁנָּפַל בַּמַּעֲרָכָה לַהֲגַנַּת הַמּוֹלֶדֶת.
הָאוֹתִיּוֹת הַקְּטַנּוֹת,
אוֹר פָּנַס הָרְחוֹב מִלֵּא אוֹתָן בְּזֹהַב לָבָן.
הֶחָוֵיר הַחַיָּל מֹשֶׁה, הֶחֱוִיר אָבִיו רָפָאֵל בֶּטֶר,
חֲקוּקִים בָּאֶבֶן,
שְׁקוּעִים בְּחַיֵּי שַׁיִשׁ.
מִתַּחַת לְפָנַס הָרְחוֹב נִפְרְשׂוּ מִטְרִיּוֹת בַּגֶּשֶׁם.
עֲנָנִים נָסְעוּ וְדָחֲפוּ זֶה אֶת זֶה לֵאמֹר:
קָדוֹשׁ!
הַגֶּשֶׁם יָרַד בְּכָל מָקוֹם,
הַגֶּשֶׁם חִלְחֵל בְּכֻלָּם בַּאֲשֶׁר הֵם שָׁם.
תנצב"ה.

הַנִּבְרֶשֶׁת הַגְּדוֹלָה הִתְנוֹדְדָה בָּרוּחַ
וְהִשְׁלִיכָה פְּרוּרֵי אוֹר
לְהַנַּדְבָנִית הַמְפֻרְסֶמֶת רָחֵל טְרַמְבֶּצְקָא
אֲשֶׁר תָּרְמָה אֶלֶף לִירָה
לַהֲקָמַת בֵּית-כְּנֶסֶת וְתַלְמוּד-תּוֹרָה.
הָאוֹתִיּוֹת הַמֻּזְהָבוֹת שֶׁל רָחֵל טְרַמְבֶּצְקָא
כְּשִׁבְּנֵי זָהָב
וּפַרְפְּרֵי לַיְלָה מְנַקְּרִים בֵּינֵיהֶן.

28

II.

The beadle, Mr. Zilberstein, locked up the Ark.
A cold wind ruffled the tennis courts and kids' trikes,
slipped through the cracks in the window pane
and flapped Sarah Beila bat Martha
who is embroidered for remembrance in the Ark's veil for all time,
flapped her and flapped her remembrance for all time
May her soul be bound in the bond of life.

Mr. Zilberstein put out the light
on the prayer leader's stand.
Night fell on the gift of Raphael Better
in memory of his soldier son Sam
who fell in the conflict to defend the motherland.
The letters caught cold,
the street lamp light filled them
with white rot.
Soldier Sam turned pale, his father Raphael Better turned pale too,
carved in the stone
sunk in the life of marble.
Beneath the street lamp light umbrellas opened in the rain.
Clouds scurried and shoved one another as if to say:
Holy!
Rain came down everywhere,
The rain rattled everyone just where they were.
May his soul be bound in the bond of life.

The big chandelier waved in the wind
and scattered crumbs of light
on the famous philanthropist Rachel Trambazke
who gave a thousand pounds
to the foundation of a house of prayer and study of sacred texts.
Rachel Trambazkae's golden letters
are like gold teeth
and night moths graze between their streaks.

מַר זִילְבֶּרְשְׁטֵיין כִּבָּה אֶת אוֹר הַנִּבְרֶשֶׁת.
תנצב''ה.

כִּסְאוֹ שֶׁל הַסַּנְדְּלָר וְכִסְאוֹ שֶׁל הַקַּצָּב
שְׁלוּבֵי זְרוֹעוֹת.
יָמִים רַבִּים חוֹרֶקֶת אַהֲבָתָם.
עַכְשָׁיו סַבָּה עֲלֵיהֶם הָאֲפֵלָה,
מֹחַ הָעֵץ הַפָּרוּעַ רוֹחֵשׁ תּוֹלָעִים.
עַל מַשְׁקוֹף דֶּלֶת הַכְּנִיסָה
כִּבָּה מַר זִילְבֶּרְשְׁטֵיין אֶת הוֹרָיו,
אֶחָיו, אַחְיוֹתָיו, דּוֹדָיו וְכָל קְרוֹבָיו
שֶׁל מַר אַהֲרֹן קוֹסְמַן
שֶׁנִּטְבְּחוּ וְשֶׁנֶּחְנְקוּ וְשֶׁנִּשְׂרְפוּ בִּידֵי הַנָּאצִים וְעוֹזְרֵיהֶם ימ''ש.
הָאוֹתִיּוֹת בַּחֹשֶׁךְ הֵן בְּכִי הַמַּעֲשִׂים.
עָמֹק בְּתוֹךְ הַחֹשֶׁךְ,
מִתַּחַת לַמְּנוֹרָה הַכְּבוּיָּה
וּמִתַּחַת לַשָּׁמַיִם נְחוּשִׁים לְהָרַע,
חָבְרוּ כָּל הָאוֹתִיּוֹת וְהָיוּ לְנָחָשׁ גָּדוֹל,
נוֹשֵׂא בְּשִׁנָּיו אֶת הַבְּרָקִים וּמַכֶּה בִּזְנָבוֹ עַל הַתְּרִיסִים
לֵאמֹר לְכָל דָּרֵי-הָאָרֶץ אֶת הוֹרָיו וְאֶת אֶחָיו
וְאֶת אַחְיוֹתָיו וְאֶת דּוֹדָיו וְאֶת כָּל קְרוֹבָיו
שֶׁל מַר אַהֲרֹן קוֹסְמַן, נְאוּם ה'.

Mr. Zilberstein put out the light of the chandelier.
May her soul be bound in the bond of life.

The chair of the cobbler and chair of the butcher
sit arm in arm.
For many a day now their love has been creaking on.
Now the dark has turned to them
the wild wood trunk is rustling with worms.
At the door jamb
Mr. Zilberstein put out the Mum and Dad,
the brothers, sisters, uncles and all known kin
of Mr. Aaron Kosman
who were butchered, strangled and burned by the Nazis
    and their kind
may their name be undone.
The letters in the dark are the sobs of deeds.
Deep in the dark
Underneath the lamp that's snuffed
and sky firm against the wrong,
all the letters joined up in a great snake
bearing in its teeth lightning and lashing its tail at the blind
to say to all that dwell in the land:
the parents and brothers and sisters and uncles and all
    known kin
of Mr Aaron Kosman, so sayeth the ineffable name.

הַסְּפַרְדִיָּה בֶּרְטָה לֵוִי כְּבָר יוֹשֶׁבֶת בַּחַלּוֹן
וּמְפַצַּחַת גַּרְעִינִים.
יַשְׁבָנֶיהָ, שְׁנֵי בְּנֵי-טוֹבִים טוֹבֵי מִשְׁקָל וְרַכֵּי בָּשָׂר
הַמִּשְׁתַּחֲוִים זֶה לָזֶה בַּחֲנֻפָּה מִדֵּי לֶכְתָּהּ
נָחִים עַכְשָׁו בְּמִשְׁקָעָם שֶׁבַּכַּרְסָה הַפַּרְחוֹנִית.
שָׁדֶיהָ, שְׁנֵי בְּנֵי-טוֹבִים סַקְרָנִים וּנְפוּחֵי אֲרֶשֶׁת,
פּוֹרְקֵי עֹל הַחֲזִיָּה, תַּמְרוּרִים לְמַאֲבַדֵּי נְתִיבָם,
מְצִיצִים עַכְשָׁו מִבַּעַד לְפֶתַח שִׂמְלָתָהּ
לִשְׁמֹעַ אֶת קְרִיאַת הַגֶּבֶר.
מַחְשְׁבוֹתֶיהָ הַבִּצְקוֹת נָאֵפוֹת לְאַט עַל רֶמֶץ מַבָּטֶיהָ.
בָּנֶיהָ אֲדֹנִי וּבֶן-גּוּרְיוֹן הָלְכוּ לְבֵית-הַסֵּפֶר
בְּנַעֲלַיִם לֹא שְׂרוּכוֹת.
בְּנוֹתֶיהָ גְלוֹרְיָה, וִיקְטוֹרְיָה וּפַנְטַסְמַגוֹרְיָה
מוֹשְׁחוֹת אֶת שְׂעָרָן בַּחֲלֵב צִפֳּרִים,
מְגָרְדוֹת פִּצְעוֹנֵי תַּאֲוָה עַל יַרְכֵיהֶן
וְשׁוֹאֲלוֹת זוֹ לָזוֹ:
מִי הָאִישׁ אֲשֶׁר אֵרַשׂ אִשָּׁה?
לְבַעֲלָהּ יוֹסֵף לֵוִי חֲנוּת נַעֲלַיִם,
הוּא אָדִיב אֵלַיִךְ בְּבוֹאֵךְ וּנְעָלָיו נִקְרָעוֹת בְּצֵאתֵךְ.
יְלָדֶיהָ סִימוֹן וְלֵיאוֹן עוֹמְדִים עַל הַגַּג בְּפִיגַ'מוֹת
וּמִשְׁתִּינִים עַל הַתַּרְנְגוֹלוֹת.
מִי זֹאת עוֹלָה מִן הָרַחְצָה?
זוֹהִי דִּינָה הַכּוֹבֶסֶת.

עַכְשָׁו, כְּשֶׁחַיִּים גּוֹרָלְנִיק מְנַשֵּׁק אֶת הַמְּזוּזָה
וְיוֹצֵא אֶת בֵּית-הַכְּנֶסֶת,
יוֹשֶׁבֶת בֶּרְטָה לֵוִי, שָׁדֶיהָ מְטַפְּסִים עַל אֶדֶן הַחַלּוֹן,
וּמְפַצַּחַת גַּרְעִינִים.
עֵינֶיהָ סוֹבְבוֹת לְאַט כִּשְׁנֵי צָבִים חוֹלִים,
רוֹאוֹת אוֹתְךָ בְּבוֹאֲךָ וּבְצֵאתְךָ וּבְלֶכְתְּךָ בַּדֶּרֶךְ,
רוֹאוֹת אֵיךְ הַגְּשָׁמִים יוֹרְדִים,
וְהַמִּנְיָן הוֹלֵךְ וּמִתְמַעֵט,
וְהַקַּדִּישׁ עוֹלֶה רָפֶה וָדַק,

III.

Spanish Berta Levi's already sitting by the window,
cracking nuts.
Her buttocks, two noble hefty weights of tender flesh
Bow to one another graciously as she walks,
Now rest in their residue, the flowered cushion.
Her breasts, two curious good-fellows with swollen faces,
Rise up against the bra, belisha beacons to those who've
    lost their way
And peep now past the gap in her dress
To hear the cry of a man.
Her doughy thoughts bake slowly on the embers of her looks.
Her sons Milord and Ben Gurion have gone to school
In shoes with both laces undone.
Her daughters Gloria, Victoria and Phantasmagoria
Anoint their hair with birds' tallow,
Scratch tiny cuts of lust on their thighs
And ask each other:
Who's the man that I will get as wife?
Her husband Joseph Levi has a shoe store
He's courtly to you as you come and his shoes crack as you go.
Her boys Simeon and Leon stand on the roof top in pyjamas
And piss on the hens.
Who is that rising from the bathroom?
That's Dina, the washerwoman.

Now, as Hayim Goralnik kisses the door scroll
And leaves the house of prayer,
Berta Levi sits, her breasts against the window pane,
Cracking nuts.
Her eyes turning slowly as two sick turtles
See you as you come and as you go and as you wend your way,
See how the rains come down
And how the quorum keeps waning,
And the mourner's prayer rises thin and faint

וְהַמִּלִּים מְסֻבָּכוֹת בְּחוּט אָדֹם,
וַאֲנָשִׁים מְעַט יוֹצְאִים אֶת בֵּית-הַכְּנֶסֶת,
מְנַשְּׁקִים אֶת הַמְּזוּזָה,
וְהַפּוֹעֵל מַדְבִּיק אֶת מוֹדָעוֹת הָאֵבֶל,
וְהָאָדָם מַרְגִּישׁ פִּתְאוֹם בְּרַע,
הוֹלֵךְ הַצִּדָּה וּמֵקִיא,
וְהַשָּׁמַיִם לוֹחֲצִים עָלָיו,
וּבְאָזְנָיו שִׁבְרֵי-תְּרוּעוֹת
כְּשֶׁהִיא יוֹשֶׁבֶת בַּחַלּוֹן וּמְפַצַּחַת גַּרְעִינִים
וּבְאָזְנָיו שִׁבְרֵי-תְּרוּעוֹת, שִׁבְרֵי-תְּרוּעוֹת.

And the words get tangled in scarlet thread
And few people go out of the house of prayer,
Kissing the door scroll,
And a workman puts up the mourning announcements
And a man feels suddenly ill
And goes to one side and throws up
And the heavens press upon him
And in his ears breaking trumpet blasts
As she sits by the window cracking nuts
And in his ears breaking trumpet blasts, breaking
    trumpet blasts.

כֶּתֶר
יִתְּנוּ לְךָ ה' אֱלֹהֵינוּ
מַלְאָכִים הֲמוֹנֵי מַעְלָה
עִם עַמְּךָ יִשְׂרָאֵל קְבוּצֵי מַטָּה.

אַחֲרֵי שֶׁכִּבָּה מַר זִילְבֶּרְשְׁטֵיין אֶת הָאוֹר
עָלָה הַלַּיְלָה כְּמוֹ קוֹל עָמֹק
צָרוּד מִכּוֹכָבִים.
לִפְנוֹת בֹּקֶר, כְּשֶׁבִּקֵּשׁ מַר שֶׁרֶשֶׁבְסְקִי לָקוּם,
לֹא נִשְׁמְעוּ לוֹ יָדָיו,
לֹא נִשְׁמְעוּ לוֹ רַגְלָיו.
הַבֹּקֶר נוֹצַק אֶל הַלַּיְלָה, הֶחָלָב אֶל הַקָּפֶה,
מַשְׁכִּימֵי קוּם וְחוֹלֵי שֶׁגֵּרוֹן
מָצְאוּ בַּשֶּׁמֶשׁ נֶחָמָה.
הַחֲבִיתוֹת הָרְחִישׁוּ, יָשְׁבֵנִי הַסְּפָרַדְיָה
צָנְחוּ אֶל הַכַּרְסָה הַפֻּרְחוֹנִית.

וִילָדִים יֵלְכוּ לְבֵית-הַסֵּפֶר, כְּבֵדִים בְּיַלְקוּטִים וּמִזְמוֹת,
וּבֵין תַּלְתַּלֵּיהֶם הַמְכֻשָּׁפָה וְעֵינֵיהֶם עוֹד קְרוּמוֹת,
וְהֶבֶל חַם יִשָּׂא בָּאֲוִיר נִיחוֹחַ לַחְמָנִיּוֹת,
וֵאלֹהִים יְשִׁיבֵנוּ אֶל יוֹמוֹ כִּימֵי עוֹלָם וּכְשָׁנִים קַדְמוֹנִיּוֹת;
גּוֹלְדְבֶּרְג, שִׁיף, וִיגְדְרְזוֹן, קוּמוּ לַעֲבוֹדַת הַבּוֹרֵא!
מְקַקְּפְסָאוֹת הַפַּח רַבִּי מֵאִיר בַּעַל הַנֵּס קוֹרֵא.

IV.

A crown
They'll give you Lord our God
Angels, the masses on high
With your people Israel gathered below.

After Mr. Zilberstein put out the light
The night rose like a deep voice
Hoarse with stars.
Towards dawn, when Mr. Shrevrevsky wanted to rise
His hands would not obey
His feet would not obey.
The morning pours into the night, the milk into the coffee.
Early risers and rheumatoid sufferers
Found in the sun a remedy.
The fried eggs whispered, the Spanish buttocks
Sank deep in the flowered cushion.

And children went to school, heavy with satchels and stratagems
A witch between their curls and eyes still crumbed with sleep
But a warm mist wafted in the air the smell of rolls
And God will return us to his day as in the days of old and
    former years;
Goldberg, Schiff, Wigderson, rise to the Creator's bidding!
Rabbi Meir master of the Miracle cries from the collection tin.

שיר מסיבת ידידים
אידיליה

בְּשָׁעָה שֶׁבַע בָּעֶרֶב בָּאִים יְדִידַי הַטּוֹבִים.
יְדֵיהֶם שְׁלוּבוֹת לְאָחוֹר. הֵם שׁוֹרְקִים שִׁירִים עֲצוּבִים,
יוֹם הָלַדְתִּי הַיּוֹם וַאֲנִי מְחַיֵּךְ מְעַט,
יְדִידַי מַקִּיפִים אוֹתִי וּמְנַעְנְעִים בְּרָאשֵׁיהֶם לְאַט,
אֲנִי אוֹמֵר לָהֶם לָשֶׁבֶת וְהֵם יוֹשְׁבִים סְבִיבִי.
אֲנִי מַבִּיט בָּהֶם וְהֵם מַבִּיטִים בִּי.

SONG OF THE PARTY OF FRIENDS
An Idyll

At seven at night my good friends come.
Their arms are held behind them. They whistle melancholy songs.
It's my birthday today and I give a little smile.
My friends ring me around and nod their heads slowly,
I tell them to sit and they sit all around.
I look at them and they look back at me.

א. מחלתה של מרת גוטמן

ד״ר בֶּרְגְמַן הָיָה נוֹתֵן בָּהּ סִימָנִים:
כְּאֵב-הָרֹאשׁ וְהַבְּחִילָה וְהַסְּחַרְחֹרֶת
וְהָרַעַד וְהַשִּׁכְחָה וְהָעִלָּפוֹן וְהַנְּפִילָה.

וּמָרַת גּוּטְמַן חוֹלָה מְאֹד
וְלֹא כִּסָּה מִמֶּנָּה הָרוֹפֵא דָּבָר.
ג' פְּעָמִים שָׁאֲלָה אִם יֵשׁ לָהּ תִּקְוָה
וְהָרוֹפֵא מְשַׂחֵק בַּגִּירוֹת עַל שֻׁלְחָנוּ.

הִיא נִסְּתָה לְהִתְעַמֵּל,
אַף נִעְנְעָה רֹאשָׁהּ בְּחָזְקָה
כִּי אָמְרָה בְּלִבָּהּ אוּלַי תִּשּׁוֹר הַמַּחֲלָה
כִּנְשֹׁר הַפְּרִי מִן הָעֵץ.
הִיא נִסְּתָה לְהָסִיחַ דַּעְתָּהּ,
הָלְכָה לַתֵּיאַטְרוֹן וְהִתְעַלְּפָה לְרַגְלֵי הַסַּדְרָן.

וְהַמַּצָּב הוֹלֵךְ הָלֹךְ וָרֵעַ
וְהַפַּחַד מְכַסֶּה אֶת כָּל הַתִּקְווֹת הַגְּבוֹהוֹת.
חָשְׁבָה מָרַת גּוּטְמַן
אוּלַי תִּקְנֶה לָהּ מִטָּה חֲדָשָׁה
וּבְרֹאשׁ הַשָּׁנָה הַחֲדָשָׁה תִּשְׁכַּב בַּמִּטָּה הַחֲדָשָׁה
וְתַתְחִיל בְּחַיִּים חֲדָשִׁים
וְהַמָּוֶת יִשְׁכַּח וְיַעֲבֹר עַל פָּנֶיהָ.
וְהַמָּוֶת יִשְׁכַּח, אֱלֹהִים שֶׁבַּשָּׁמַיִם, יִשְׁכַּח.

בִּשְׁמוֹנָה בָּעֶרֶב הָיְתָה הַתְּקָפָה קָשָׁה.
נִשְׁעֶנֶת עַל כָּתֵף בְּנוֹתֶיהָ יָרְדָה לְהָקִיא
וּבַעֲלָה מְדַלֵּג לִפְנֵיהֶן לִפְתֹּחַ אֶת הַדְּלָתוֹת.
עָבְרָה חִוֶּרֶת מְאֹד וּמִתְנוֹדֶדֶת
עַל פְּנֵי תְמוּנָה וּשְׁתֵּי כֻּרְסוֹת
וְהִגִּיעָה אֶל בֵּית-הַכִּסֵּא.
הִדְּקָה הַבַּת הָאַחַת אֶת כַּף יָדָהּ אֶל מִצְחָהּ
וּמָרַת גּוּטְמַן הֵקִיאָה אֶל תּוֹךְ הָאַסְלָה הַמַּבְרִיקָה.

I. MRS. GUTMAN'S DISEASE

Dr. Bergman would give her acronyms:
Headache and nausea and dizzy spells
And shakes and forgetfulness and fainting and falling down.
And Mrs. Gutman is very ill
And the doctor did not keep a thing from her.
Three times she asked if there was a chance
And the doctor played with papers on his desk.

She tried exercise
Even shook her head vigorously
For she said in her heart of hearts
Maybe the illness will fall away
As a fruit falls from a branch.
To try and take her mind off it
She went to the theatre
And fainted at the usher's feet.

But the situation keeps getting worse
And fear covers up all the high hopes.
Mrs. Marta Gutman thought
Maybe she'd buy a new mattress
And as the New Year starts, she'd lie on the new mattress
And start a new existence
And it would slip death's mind
And he'd pass her by.
And it would slip death's mind, God in heaven, slip his mind.

At eight in the evening there was another bad attack.
She leaned on her daughters' shoulders and went downstairs to puke
With her husband skipping ahead, opening all the doors.
She passed very pale and swayed
Before the pictures and two armchairs
And got to the littlest room.
One daughter pressed her hand to her brow
And Mrs. Gutman heaved into the gleaming bowl.

דָּם רַב מִן הָרָאוֹת נִשְׁפַּךְ בְּקִיאָהּ,
וְהַגְּנִיחוֹת עֲמֻקּוֹת וּשְׁבוּרוֹת,
וּמַר גּוּטְמַן נוֹשֵׁךְ אֶת שְׂפָתוֹ הַתַּחְתּוֹנָה
וּמַבִּיט אֲחוֹרָה אֶל הַשְּׁכֵנוֹת הַנִּקְבָּצוֹת
וְהֵן מַבִּיטוֹת אֵלָיו.
וּבְשָׁפְכָהּ מָרַת גּוּטְמַן אֶת דָּמָהּ הַחוּצָה
זָכְרָה אֶת הַמִּטָּה הַחֲדָשָׁה
וְזָכְרָה אֶת הַחַיִּים הַחֲדָשִׁים,
אָז הֵסַבָּה רֹאשָׁהּ אֶל הַשְּׁכֵנוֹת הַנִּקְבָּצוֹת,
וְעֵינֶיהָ כִּמְעַט עֲצוּמוֹת וּבְנוֹתֶיהָ מְנַגְּבוֹת אֶת מִצְחָהּ,
וְשָׁאֲלָה בְּקוֹל רָפֶה לָמָּה לֹא בָּא הַנַּגָּר,
וְהַשְּׁכֵנָה הָרִאשִׁית מְשִׁיבָה 'עוֹד מְעַט',
וְאַחַר־כָּךְ שָׁבָה מָרַת גּוּטְמַן לְהָקִיא,
וּבֵין דָּם לְדָם קָרְאָה 'אֵיפֹה הַנַּגָּר',
וְהַשְּׁכֵנוֹת מִתְגּוֹדְדוֹת מֵאֲחוֹרֶיהָ וְצוֹחֲקוֹת צְחוֹק מַר.

בְּשֶׁבַע וָחֵצִי בָּעֶרֶב נִדְלָקִים פַּנְסֵי הָרְחוֹב,
גְּבָרִים שְׁלוּבֵי גְּבָרוֹת יוֹצְאִים לַחֲפֵשׂ טוֹב,
יוֹצֵאת הָאַלְמָנָה הַמְחֻקֶּנֶת, יוֹצֵא אִישׁ נִשְׁבָּר,
אָנוּ יוֹשְׁבִים בְּשֶׁקֶט וְאֵינֶנּוּ אוֹמְרִים דָּבָר,
יְדִידַי מְנַגְּבִים בְּמִטְפָּחוֹת אֶת הַזֵּעָה מִצַּוָּארָם,
הֵם מְנַפְנְפִים בָּעִתּוֹנִים עַל בָּתֵּי־שֶׁחְיָם.

Lots of blood out of the lungs spilled in her vomit
And the deep, broken groans
And Mr. Gutman bites his lower lip
And looks back at the neighbours gathering
And they look back at him.
And while Mrs. Gutman poured her blood out
She remembered the new mattress
Then she turned her head to the gathered neighbours' wives
And her eyes nearly closed and her daughters wiped her brow,
And she asked in a faint voice
Why the carpenter hadn't arrived
And the closest neighbour replied "soon"
And then Mrs. Gutman heaved up again,
And in between blood and blood
She called "Where's the carpenter?"
And the neighbours crowd round behind her and laugh a
   bitter laugh.

At seven thirty at night the street lamps are lit
Guys entwined with gals go out to seek what's neat,
A fixed widow goes out, the broken man goes forth
We sit quietly and do not say a word,
My friends wipe with handkerchiefs the sweat from their necks,
They wave newspapers under their armpits.

ב. מות גיסו של במברג

יְדִידִי, הֲשָׁכַחְתָּ אֶת מוֹדָעוֹת הָאֵבֶל?
בַּחֲצִי הַלַּיְלָה רָץ בַּמְבֶּרְג אֶל הַדְּפוּס,
וּבְרַעַשׁ הַמְּכוֹנָה הִגִּיד אֶת שֵׁם גִּיסוֹ וְגִילוֹ
וְשֵׁם אָבִיו וְשֵׁם עִירוֹ הַחֲרֵבָה
וְטִיב מוֹתוֹ וּמוֹעֵד לְוָיָתוֹ,
וְהַפּוֹעֵל הָרָזֶה הָיָה מְנַעְנֵעַ בְּרֹאשׁוֹ כִּי שָׁמַע
וְאֶצְבְּעוֹתָיו מְצָרְפוֹת בָּעוֹפֶרֶת, אוֹת לְאוֹת,
אֶת שֵׁם גִּיסוֹ הַמֵּת שֶׁל בַּמְבֶּרְג.

הִזָּהֲרוּ מִפְּנֵי הַפּוֹעֵל הָרָזֶה,
כִּי בְּצָרֵף אֶצְבְּעוֹתָיו אֶת שִׁמְכֶם בָּעוֹפֶרֶת
תִּהְיוּ מֵתִים גְּמוּרִים.

לִפְנֵי עֲלוֹת הַשַּׁחַר הָאֲוִיר עוֹדֶנּוּ צוֹנֵן,
מַדְבִּיק מוֹדָעוֹת הָאֵבֶל רוֹכֵב עַל אוֹפַנָּיו,
חָג סְבִיב בֵּית הַמֵּת,
עוֹשֶׂה כְּנָפַיִם לִבְשׂוֹרַת מוֹתוֹ,
שָׁף בְּיָדָיו לְחַמְּמָן, מַחְשְׁבוֹתָיו קָרוֹת וַעֲיֵפוֹת.

וְלִפְעָמִים יַעֲבֹר הַשּׁוֹטֵר אוֹ מֵרִיק הַפַּחִים,
וְיִרְאֶה אֶת הַדְּלִי וְהַדֶּבֶק וְהַמִּבְרֶשֶׁת
וּמֵאָה מוֹדָעוֹת הָאֵבֶל עַל גִּיסוֹ הַמֵּת שֶׁל בַּמְבֶּרְג,
וְהַמַּדְבִּיק מְשַׂמֵּחַ אֶת לִבּוֹ הַקַּר
בְּזֶמֶר פָּרְסִי עַתִּיק.

כְּמוֹ שֶׁעוֹלָה הַצְּעָקָה מִן הַכְּאֵב,
עוֹלֶה הַבֹּקֶר מִתּוֹךְ הַלַּיְלָה.
קָם הַתַּרְנְגוֹל וְהֵעִיר אֶת הַשְּׁכֵנָה.
קָמָה הַשְּׁכֵנָה וּפָהֲקָה הַשָּׁמַיְמָה
וּפָתְחָה אֶת הַתְּרִיסִים
וְרָאֲתָה כִּי הַלַּיְלָה פָּלַט מֵתִים.

II. THE DEATH OF BAMBERG'S BROTHER-IN-LAW

My friend, have you forgotten the mourning announcements?
At midnight Bamberg ran to the press
And in the din of the machine
Told his brother-in-law's name and age
And his father's name and name of his ruined city of origin
And the cause of death and the burial place
And the thin workman shook his head as he listened
And his fingers joined in lead, letter by letter
The name of Bamberg's brother-in-law, deceased.
Beware of the thin workman
For when his fingers join your name in lead
You'll be as dead as dirt.

Before dawn rose, the air still chill
The mourning notice sticker rides his bicycle,
Circles round the deceased's house in a radius
Giving wings to the news of his passing,
Chafing his hands to warm them up, his thoughts cold
    and weary.

And sometimes a policeman goes by or a garbage man
And he'll see the pail and the glue and the brush
And a hundred mourning announcements
About Bamberg's brother-in-law
And the notice sticker gladdens his cold heart
With an ancient Persian tune.
Just as the shout comes from pain
Morning rises from night.
The cock rose and woke the neighbour
She got up and yawned to the sky
And opened up the blinds
And saw the night had disgorged dead.

שׁוֹתִים תֵּה בִּדְמָמָה בְּאוֹר צָהֹב וְדַל,
אֲשֶׁר הִתְקִינָה לְהָאִיר אֶת עֵינֵינוּ חֶבְרַת הַחַשְׁמַל,
בְּשָׁעָה עֶשֶׂר בָּעֶרֶב רוֹעֶה הַזּוֹנוֹת יוֹצֵא,
מְחַלֵּל שִׁירֵי עֹנֶג, מוֹלִיךְ נַעֲרוֹתָיו לַמִּרְעֶה,
אַחַת קְטַנָּה וּשְׁחֹרָה, הַשְּׁנִיָּה בֵּינוֹנִית וּצְהֻבָּה,
גּוֹעוֹת לְעֵבֶר הַיָּם, בְּעֶצֶב אוֹהֲבוֹת אַהֲבָה.

46

We drink tea in silence by gold, dull light
Installed to light our eyes by the nuclear plant,
At ten at night the whore shepherd ventures forth
Piping songs of joy, leading his girls to grass
One small and dark, the second middling and sallow
Lowing toward the sea, sadly they love, love.

ג. הלוויתו של אברהם צדר

הִנֵּה קְרֵבוֹת הַמַּצֵּבוֹת.
הָעֵצִים הַיְרֻקִּים חוֹפִים עַל הָאֶבֶן
וְהָאֶבֶן מְכֻסָּה עַל הַגּוּפוֹת.
הַכֹּל מֻנָּח בִּמְקוֹמוֹ
וְהַשַּׁלְוָה רַבָּה.
הֻפְשַׁט אַבְרָהָם צֶדֶר,
נָקִי וְעָטוּף בְּטַלִּית
יִשָּׂאוּהוּ אַרְבָּעָה אֲנָשִׁים,
לְפָנָיו הַחַזָּן הַמְזַמֵּר
וְאַחֲרָיו הַנָּשִׁים הַבּוֹכִיּוֹת,
וּבָאֶמְצַע מוּטָל הוּא,
חֲתַן הָאֵבֶל בִּכְבוֹדוֹ וּבְעַצְמוֹ.
הַקַּבְּרָן קוֹפֵץ אֶל הַבּוֹר,
אֶת הַמֵּת יָרִים בִּזְרוֹעוֹתָיו
וְיַנִּיחַ אוֹתוֹ בַּבּוֹר.

אָנוּ הוֹלְכִים אֶל הָאֲדָמָה,
זִכְרוּ אֶת מַעֲשֵׂינוּ הַטּוֹבִים,
חִשְׁבוּ עָלֵינוּ לִפְרָקִים,
אֵיךְ הָיִינוּ גַּם אָנוּ בָּאוֹר
וְעַכְשָׁו נִזְרַעְנוּ בַּחֹשֶׁךְ
לְזַמֵּר אֶת פְּרִי מַעֲשֵׂינוּ לִפְנֵי הָאֱלֹהִים.

וּבְבוֹא הַמָּשִׁיחַ
יִפָּתְחוּ הַקְּבָרִים, קֶבֶר קֶבֶר לְאִישׁ,
וְהַמֵּת יָקוּם וִימַצְמֵץ בְּעֵינָיו,
וִינַעֵר אֶת הָאָבָק מִכְּנַף טַלִּיתוֹ,
אָז יָקוּמוּ כֻּלָּם שֶׁלִּוִּינוּ לְעוֹלָמָם,
יָקוּם הֻפְשַׁט אַבְרָהָם צֶדֶר,
יָקוּמוּ אָבִיו וְאָבִיו-זְקֵנוֹ,
וְכָל אֲבוֹתֵינוּ אֲשֶׁר צִוּוּ לָנוּ אֶת מוֹתָם.
וְכָל הַנְּעָרִים יַעֲלוּ וְיַעַמְדוּ,
וּבֵין הָעַרְבַּיִם הָאֲוִיר מָתוֹק,

III. THE FUNERAL OF ABRAHAM ZEDER

Here come the monuments.
The green trees canopy the stone
And the stone covers the remains.
Everything is laid in its proper place
And the peace is great.
The deceased, Abraham Zeder
Clean and wrapped in a prayer shawl
Will be borne by four men
Before him the cantor singing,
And after him the women weeping
And in the middle will be thrown down him,
The mourning bridegroom in all his glory.
The grave digger jumps into the hole
And lifts the dead man in his arms
And lays him into the earth.

We walk on the earth,
Remember our good deeds,
Think of us at intervals,
How we too were in the light
And now are sown in darkness
To sing the harvest of our deeds before the Lord.

And when Messiah comes
They'll open the graves, grave by grave for each man
And the dead man will rise and blink
And shake the dust from his prayer shawl band
Then will rise all that came with us to their end,
The deceased Abraham Zeder will rise again,
His Dad and granddad will rise too
And all our fathers who left us their deaths as an estate.
And all the boys will rise and stand
And at twilight the air is sweet,

וְכָל הַמֵּתִים יִשְׁתָּאוּ לִרְאוֹת
אֵיךְ גָּדְלוּ הָעֵצִים וְהָאֲפִירָה מַצַּבְתָּם,
וְעוֹד יַבִּיטוּ וְיִשְׁתָּאוּ זֶה אֶל זֶה
וְהַמָּשִׁיחַ עוֹבֵר בֵּינֵיהֶם וְצוֹחֵק
וּמְחַלֵּק סָכָּרִיּוֹת מֶנְתָּה.

צוֹפִים מִבַּעַד לַחַלּוֹן אֵיךְ כָּבִים אוֹרוֹת הַבָּתִּים.
הוֹלְכֵי לִישׁוֹן בַּלַּיְלָה, לֹא כֻלָּם בַּבֹּקֶר קָמִים,
מִי יִתְהַפֵּךְ עַל מִשְׁכָּבוֹ, וּמִי תָּבוֹא עָלָיו מַהְפֵּכָה,
מִי יֵרֵד לְהָקִיא בַּחֹשֶׁךְ, וּמִי תֵּרֵד עָלָיו הַחֲשֵׁכָה.
בְּשָׁעָה שְׁתֵּים-עֶשְׂרֵה בַּלַּיְלָה כָּבִים פְּנָסֵי הָרְחוֹב,
יְדִידַי וַאֲנִי מַבִּיטִים וְרוֹאִים כִּי לֹא טוֹב.

50

And all the dead will wonder
How tall the trees have grown and how grey their grave,
And still they'll look and wonder at themselves
And Messiah pass among them and laugh
Handing out to each of them a mint cough drop.

Looking out the window
As the house lights go out.
Those that go to sleep at night, don't all get up,
Who will turn on his couch and who be overturned,
Who go down to heave in the dark
And who have dark on him descend.
At midnight the street lights go out
My friends and I look
And see all is not good.

ה. סוֹף דָּבָר

אַחֲרֵי הַחֲתֻנּוֹת וְהַשְּׂמָחוֹת
וְהַמְּצוּקָה וְהַתְּפִלָּה וְהָרֶוַח וְהָעֱנוּת
וּתְפִלַּת הָעֲנִיִּים וּבִרְכַּת הָעֲשִׁירִים,
הִנֵּה בָּא הַסּוֹף,
וְהוּא רַע יוֹתֵר מִשֶּׁחָשַׁבְנוּ
וְרַע יוֹתֵר לֹא יָכוֹל לִהְיוֹת.
מִי הָאִישׁ אֲשֶׁר בָּנָה בַּיִת חָדָשׁ
יֵלֵךְ וְיָשֹׁב אֶל סוֹפוֹ;
מִי הָאִישׁ אֲשֶׁר נָטַע כֶּרֶם
יֵלֵךְ וְיָשֹׁב אֶל סוֹפוֹ;
מִי הָאִישׁ אֲשֶׁר אֵרַשׂ לוֹ אִשָּׁה
יֵלֵךְ וְיָשֹׁב אֶל סוֹפוֹ;
מִי הָאִישׁ הַיָּרֵא וְרַךְ-הַלֵּבָב
יֵלֵךְ גַּם הוּא וְיָשֹׁב אֶל סוֹפוֹ.

וְכָל הַמְּקַרְקְעִין יִהְיוּ מִטַּלְטְלִין בְּרוּחַ עַזָּה.
וְכָל הַמְּקַרְקְעִין יִהְיוּ מִטַּלְטְלִין בְּרוּחַ עַזָּה.
וְכָל הַמְּקַרְקְעִין יִהְיוּ מִטַּלְטְלִין בְּרוּחַ עַזָּה.

יֵשׁ אֵפוֹא מָקוֹם לְיֵאוּשׁ מֻחְלָט,
לְשֵׁנָה אֲרֻכָּה וְלַחֲלוֹמוֹת זִמָּה,
לְשִׁירֵי הֶפְקֵר וּלְהוֹנָאַת הַחֶנְוָנִים,
לְיִדּוּי אֲבָנִים בְּזִקְנָה וָגֵו,
לַעֲזִיבַת הַנַּחֲלָאוֹת וְלִשְׁמִיטַת חֲפָצִים קְטַנִּים.

וּבְכֵן, רֵעִים חַיֵּינוּ, רַע מוֹתֵנוּ,
אָבְדָה תִּקְוָתֵנוּ.

אֲנִי מְנַגֵּב אֶת מִצְחִי, בַּחַלּוֹן הַיָּרֵחַ עוֹלֶה
וְהוּא נָפוּחַ, מְסֹאָב בִּכְתָמִים וְחוֹלֶה,
יְדִידַי קָמִים עָלַי בִּצְוָחַת עוֹפוֹת שְׁחוּטִים,
דָּם שָׁחֹר וְחָמוּץ מֵצִיף אֶת פְּנֵי הַשִּׂרְטוּטִים,
וְעִמָּנוּ הַזַּמֶּרֶת הַשְּׁמֵנָה וְהִיא מְזִיעָה פְּלָגִים,
אָנוּ עוֹלִים עַל יַרְכָתֶיהָ, זוֹקְפִים אֶת הַתֹּרֶן וּמַפְלִיגִים.

52

IV. CLOSE OF THE DAY

After the weddings and celebrations
And the deprivation and meditation and relief and misery
And the exhortations of the poor and blessing of the rich,
Here comes the end,
And it is worse than we anticipated
And there is no way it could be worse than this.
Who is the man who built a new house,
Let him go and return to his end,
Who is the man who planted his vine,
Let him go and return to his end,
Who is the man who betrothed him a wife,
Let him go and return to his end;
Who is the man who's fearful and soft at heart
Let him too go back to his end.

And all the fixtures will be as fittings in a great wind.
And all the fixtures will be as fittings in a great wind.
And all the fixtures will be as fittings in a great wind.

There is therefore cause for absolute despair,
For a long sleep and dreams of lechery
For wanton singing and defrauding of grocers
For throwing stones at old ladies and Quasimodos,
For abandonment of bequests and throwing off of small matters.

And so, our lives are ill, and our deaths are ill.
And lost all of our day dreams.

> I mop my brow, in the window a moon ascends
> Swollen, stained and sickly,
> My friends rise against me with the cry of slaughtered hens,
> Black sour blood floods my scoured face,
> And the fat singer is with us and she's sweating rivers
> We board onto her stern, raise the mast and set sail.

חיי המתים
פואמה

שְׁמֶעְר'ל, מוֹכֵר לְבֶּעְר'ל,
וּבֶעְר'ל קוֹנֶה מִגֶּעצְ'ל,
וּבְתוֹךְ כֻּלָּם, כְּמוֹ חוֹר בְּתוֹךְ בֵּייגְ'ל
הַקֵּץ, הַמְכַנֶּה גַּם קֶצְ'ל.

LIVES OF THE DEAD
An Epic

Shmerl sells to Berl,
and Berl buys from Getzl.
And inside of them all
like a hole inside the bagel
is death, also known as Detzl.

פרק ראשון

וְהָאִישׁ הַמֵּת שָׁכַב בָּעֲגָלָה
חִוֵּר מֵעֶלְבּוֹן אֵין-אוֹנִים.
וְהוּא מְחֻתָּל כְּתִינוֹק בְּחִתּוּלָיו
לְלֹא מִכְנָסַיִם, בְּלֹא תַּחְתּוֹנִים,

תִּשְׁפָּתָיו מְתוּחוֹת בַּעֲוִית בּוּשָׁה:
אֵינֶנִּי יָכוֹל עוֹד לְסַפֵּק אִשָּׁה.

עֵירֹם וְעֶרְיָה, לְלֹא מִכְנָסַיִם, בְּלֹא מְעִיל,
רַק עָטוּף בְּבַד לָבָן, כְּתִינוֹק מְחֻתָּל בְּחִתּוּלָיו,
הֻנַּח הָאִישׁ הַמֵּת עַל הָעֲגָלָה הַצָּרָה
הַמִּתְגַּלְגֶּלֶת לְאַט בִּשְׁבִיל הֶעָפָר.

וְלִפְנֵי הָעֲגָלָה הוֹלֵךְ הַחַזָּן הַמְזַמֵּר, לָבוּשׁ מִכְנָסַיִם,
לוֹעֵס בְּקוֹלוֹ הֶחָרֵב חֲצִיר תְּפִלָּה יְבֵשָׁה,
וְאַחֲרֵי הָעֲגָלָה הוֹלֶכֶת הָאִשָּׁה הַבּוֹכִיָּה עֲטוּיַת הַשְּׁחֹרִים,
וּפָנֶיהָ נְפוּחִים וַאֲדֻמִּים כִּפְנֵי הַמִּתְאַמֵּץ בְּבֵית-כִּסֵּא,
וְקֹמֶץ גְּבָרִים סוֹבְבִים אוֹתָהּ חֶרֶשׁ בְּאשֶׁת מִכְנָסַיִם,
וּמְנִידִים רָאשֵׁיהֶם, וְנוֹפְחִים מֵעֵת לְעֵת בְּאַפָּם.

עַל שְׂפַת הַבּוֹר הֻצַּג הַמֵּת לְרַאֲוָה, וְהָיְתָה דּוּמִיָּה.
וְהָאִישׁ הַמֵּת יָדַע וְיָדְעוּ כֻלָּם כִּי אֵינֶנּוּ עוֹד גֶּבֶר,
וְכִי מִכְנָסָיו הַיְקָרִים נִשְׁלְלוּ מִמֶּנּוּ לָעַד,
וּלְאוֹת כִּי לְעוֹלָם לֹא יָפִיק עוֹד אֲנָקַת תַּעֲנוּג מִגְּרוֹן הָאִשָּׁה
עָטְפוּ אוֹתוֹ בְּחִתּוּל הַתִּינוֹק הַלָּבָן.

CHAPTER ONE

And the dead man lay in the cart
pale with shame and helplessness,
and diapered like an infant in his diapers
without trousers and without underpants.

And his lips taut in a twist of disgrace:
I can no longer satisfy a woman.

Completely starkers, no coat and no trousers,
just wrapped in a white sheet, like a baby wrapped in diapers,
here lies the dead man on the narrow cart
that strolls slowly down the path of dust.

And before the cart walks the cantor and sings, wearing
     his trousers
chewing with his dry stalk voice dry prayers,
and after the cart comes a woman, weeping in widow's weeds,
and her face swollen and red as the face of one straining in
     the jakes,
and a handful of men hang around her in a murmur of trousers,
and nod their heads and honk from time to time their schnozzles.

At the lip of the hole the dead man was displayed and there
     was silence.
And the dead man knew and they all knew he was a man
     no longer,
for his dear trousers had been stripped from him for ever,
as a mark that he would never again
evince a groan of pleasure from the throat of woman
they wrapped him in the baby's white nappy cotton.

וְכַאֲשֶׁר שְׁמָטוּהוּ בְּחִתּוּל הַתִּינוֹק הַלָּבָן אֶל תַּחְתִּית הַבּוֹר
הָיוּ שִׂפְתֵי הָאִישׁ הַמֵּת חֲרוּרוֹת מֵעֶלְבּוֹן נוֹרָא
וּמְתוּחוֹת אָחוֹרָה בַּעֲוִית חִיּוּךְ מִתְנַצֵּל,
וְהָיָה לוֹ צֹרֶךְ עַז לִבְלֹעַ רֻקּוֹ מֵעֶלְבּוֹן, אַךְ פִּיו הָיָה יָבֵשׁ.

פִּי הַחַי שׁוֹפֵעַ רֹק, יֵשׁ לוֹ דַּי לְמוֹסֵס וְלִשְׁטֹף אֶל קִרְבּוֹ
חֲזִירִים וְדָגִים וְעוּגוֹת, וְעוֹד נוֹתָר לוֹ גַּם לִירֹק הַחוּצָה עַל רֵעָיו;
וּפִי הַמֵּת יָבֵשׁ, אֵין לוֹ כְּדֵי לִבְלֹעַ חֶרֶשׁ אֶת חֶרְפַּת מוֹתוֹ.

וְגֹבַהּ פְּנֵי הַגֶּבֶר הַמֵּת נָמוּךְ מִגֹּבַהּ פִּי עֶרְוַת הָאִשָּׁה הַחַיָּה,
וְנִמְצָא בְּמַעֲבֶה הָאֲדָמָה עַל מִישׁוֹר תְּעָלוֹת הַבִּיּוּב, שָׁם נִסְפַּח הַמֵּת
אֶל כָּל צְבָא הַמֵּתִים הַמְטֻמְטָם הַשּׁוֹכֵב בָּאֲפֵלָה, גְּוִו מָתוּחַ,
שׁוֹמֵר בְּמִסְדָּר נִצְחִי עַל הַטִּנֹּפֶת וְעַל הַסִּרָחוֹן שֶׁל מַחְסְנֵי הַשּׁוֹפְכִין הָאַדִּירִים.

קוּם הִתְגַּיֵּס לַמָּוֶת, צֵא אֶל הַהַרְפַּתְקָה,
לֵךְ לְהַסְרִיחַ דָּם, שְׁכַב מֻשְׁפָּל וּמִתְרַפֵּס
בְּמַחֲנֶה עֲנָק שֶׁל צִיּתָנוּת עֲוֶרֶת,
לֵךְ לְהָגֵן בָּאֲפֵלָה עַל תַּרְמִילֵי הַפְּסֹלֶת
שֶׁל הָאִשָּׁה אֲשֶׁר הוֹתַרְתְּ מֵעָלֶיךָ,
אֲשֶׁר הִיא מוֹרִידָה אֵלֶיךָ בֹּקֶר בֹּקֶר,
עִם קְצָת מַיִם עֲכוּרִים, לַבּוֹר.

58

And when they cast him in the baby's white nappy down
      to the hole's bottom
the dead man's lips were pale with the terrible humiliation
and stretched backward in the rictus of an apologetic grin
and he had a fierce need to swallow the bile of his shame,
      but his mouth was all dry.

The mouth of the living is awash with spit, it has enough to
      melt and wash within it
pigs and fish and cakes and still have enough to spit at friends;
and the dead man's dry mouth has not enough to silently
      swallow the disgrace of his death.

And the level of the dead man's mouth is set below the living
      woman's crotch
and is found in the thick of the earth on the plateau of the
      sewage pipes
there the deceased is joined to all the dumb host of the dead
that lie in the darkness, stretched on their backs
keeping the eternal watch on the filth and stink of the great
      warehouses of shit.

Rise and join up with death, set off on the great adventure,
go stink at attention, lie debased and grovelling
in the great boot camp of blind obedience,
go defend in darkness the kit bags of refuse
of the woman that you left overhead,
that she lowers down to you dawn by dawn
with a little cloudy water, through the hole.

לַיְלָה, דּוּמִיָּה. רַק קוֹל תְּסִיסָה שֶׁל הַגּוּפוֹת הַנִּרְקָבִים,
כְּמוֹ הֲמִיָּה בִּלְתִּי פּוֹסֶקֶת, וּפֹה וָשָׁם מִלְּמַעְלָה נוֹבֵחַ בֵּית־כִּסֵּא,
פֶּרֶץ מַיִם בָּאַסְלָה שׁוֹצֵף לוֹ כְּמוֹ צְחוֹק פִּרְאֵי לַעַג, מָלֵא חַיִּים,
וְהוֹף, זֶהֲמָה נִבְלַעַת בַּצִּנּוֹר, יוֹרֶדֶת מַטָּה,
אַחֲרֶיהָ מִין גִּרְגּוּר נִמְשָׁךְ שֶׁל מַיִם חֲדָשִׁים אֶל הָאַסְלָה,
כְּמוֹ לֹא הָיְתָה לוֹ רְוָיָה לַצְּחוֹק, וְהוּא מוֹסִיף קְצָת חִי־חִי־חִי
מוּל פְּנֵי הַמֵּת הַמְבַקֵּשׁ לִבְלֹעַ רַק וּפִיו יָבֵשׁ, מֻקָּף בְּבֹשֶׁת וּבִסְחִי.

תְּנֻעַת הָאִשָּׁה הַשְּׁקִיפָה בְּיֹבֶשׁ
אֵיךְ מוּרָד הַמֵּת לְהַצְחִין
אַרְבַּע אַמּוֹת תַּחַת כַּפּוֹת רַגְלֶיהָ,
עַל מִישׁוֹר אֶחָד עִם תְּעָלוֹת הַשּׁוֹפְכִין.

וַאֲחוֹרֵי הָאִשָּׁה בְּבֵית־הַכִּסֵּא
יִהְיוּ מֵעָלָיו כְּמוֹ גְזַר־דִּין מִתְנַשֵּׂא.

Night time, silence. Just the fermenting sound of bodies rotting,
like an unceasing moan, and from here and there above the
    bark of a toilet,
a burst of water in the bowl streams like wild mocking
    laughter, full of living
and Bob's your uncle, filth goes down the chute, slides down
after it a kind of gurgle of new water in the bowl
as if it hadn't had its fill of laughing, and adds a little chortle
in the face of the deceased who wants to swallow spit
while his mouth is dry, surrounded by shame and debris.

And the crotch of the woman gazed drily
as the dead man was lowered to stink
four yards beneath the soles of her feet
on one level with the sewage lines

and the woman's rear in the smallest room
will be above him like a sentence for all time.

פרק שני

וְהָאִישׁ אָמַר, מַה נּוֹתַר לוֹ לַמֵּת
אִם לֹא לִהְיוֹת פִּילוֹסוֹף,
זְמַן לְמַכְבִּיר נִתַּן לִי כָּאן
אֶת חִידַת הַחַיִּים הָעֲמֻקָה לַחֲשֹׂף.

הֵצִיץ הָאִישׁ אֶל תּוֹכוֹ וְיָדַע:
בַּחַיִּים הָאֵלֶּה אֵין שׁוּם חִידָה.

בַּחֲשֵׁכַת הַבּוֹר הָאָטוּם, בָּעוֹלָם הַקָּטָן הֶעָגוּם שֶׁל רִקְבוֹן בְּשָׂרוֹ
מְנַהֵל הָאִישׁ הַמֵּת אֶת חַיֵּי מוֹתוֹ הָאֻמְלָל.
וּכְפִי שֶׁיִּקְרֶה לְאָדָם הַיָּשֵׁן בְּפֶה פָּעוּר וְחוֹלֵם חֲלוֹם,
וּמַכָּר בֶּן חַיִל מִתְיַצֵּב לְפֶתַע מֵעָלָיו, מַפְשִׁיל מִכְנָסַיִם,
וּמַטִּיל אֶת צְרָכָיו לְתוֹךְ פִּיו מַעֲשֵׂה לָצוֹן,
וְהָאָדָם הַיָּשֵׁן קוֹפֵץ מִמְּקוֹמוֹ בְּתִמָּהוֹן מַכְאוֹב
וּמְנַעֵר אֶת רֹאשׁוֹ וְיוֹרֵק וּמוֹחֶה אֶת הַטֻּנֶּפֶת מִפִּיו,
וּלְרֶגַע מוּאָר לְעֵינָיו הָעוֹלָם הָאֱנוֹשִׁי בְּנֹגַהּ צוֹרֵב, מַחֲלִיא,
כָּךְ נִדְחָס הַבֹּץ וְנִגְרִים הַמַּיִם וּמְמַלְאִים
אֶת חֲלַל פִּיו הַפָּעוּר לִרְוָחָה שֶׁל הָאִישׁ הַמֵּת,
וְהָאִישׁ הַמֵּת אֵינֶנּוּ קוֹפֵץ וְאֵינֶנּוּ יוֹרֵק וְאֵינֶנּוּ מוֹחֶה,
וְרַק תִּמָּהוֹן הַמַּכְאוֹב עַל פָּנָיו לֹא יֶחְדָּל.

וְהָאִישׁ הַמֵּת חָלָה מֵרֹב צַעַר וְרֹגֶז וּבְשָׂרוֹ נַעֲשָׂה רָזֶה,
וּשְׂפָתָיו הַחִוְּרוֹת גָּאֶכְלוּ מִמִּסְגֶּרֶת פִּיו, וּבֶחָיוּךְ נִבְזֶה נֶחְשְׂפוּ שִׁנָּיו,
וּכְכָל שֶׁנִּסָּה לִסְגֹּר אֶת חִיּוּכוֹ, חִיּוּךְ הַמֵּת הַנִּכְלָם, הַמִּתְנַצֵּל,
וְלָעֲטוֹת עַל פָּנָיו אֲרֶשֶׁת חֲמוּרָה וְחָרוֹן כַּיָּאֶה לְבַעַל סֵבֶל,
כָּךְ הָלְכוּ שִׁנָּיו וְנֶחְשְׂפוּ, וְרָחַב הַחִיּוּךְ, וְהִשְׂתָּרַע מֵאֹזֶן לְאֹזֶן,

CHAPTER TWO

And the man said, what has the dead man left
if not to be philosophical,
I've plenty of time here at my disposal
to solve the deep meaning of it all.

The man peeked in himself and knew
in this life there is no riddle.

In the darkness of a sealed hole, in the small sad world of his
flesh's dispersal
the dead man manages his miserable dead existence.
And as will happen to a man asleep with his mouth open who
dreams a dream
so a friendly wise guy stops of a sudden overhead and drops
his pants to take a leak
in his mouth for a lark
and the sleeping man leaps up in pained surprise
and shakes his head and spits and wipes the ordure from his mouth
and for a moment the human world is lit before him with a
burning glow, nauseating
thus the mud is stuffed and the water drawn to fill
the hollow in the open mouth of the dead man
and the dead man does not jump and does not spit and does
not protest,
and only the pained surprise on his face does not fade.

And the dead man got sick with sorrow and his flesh wasted away
and his pale lips ate back from the rim of his mouth, and his
teeth bared a foolish grin
and for all he tried to shut his grin, that smile of the
embarrassed dead, apologetic,
to swathe his face in a severe frown of wrath as befits one in pain,
the more his teeth unveiled, and the grin broadened, and
stretched from ear to ear

63

וְהָיָה לַעֲוִית גְּחוּךְ מִתְרַפֵּס שֶׁל חֲדַל אִישִׁים.
כָּל הַמֵּתִים שׁוֹכְבִים פַּרְקְדָן, מְגַחֲכִים בְּהִתְרַפְּסוּת כְּלַפֵּי מַעְלָה,
כְּאִלּוּ רָאוּ מֵעֲלֵיהֶם אֶת הַתִּקְרָה הַמְנֻצַּחַת,
כְּמוֹ עֲדַת הַנָּשִׁים הַמְכַעֲרוֹת הַמְגֻחֲכוֹת בְּמֶסִבַּת רִקּוּדִים
לַהֲלָצָה גְּרוּעָה שֶׁל גֶּבֶר שָׁמֵן לֹא אָמִיד, וּבְלִבָּן טִינָה.

וְהָאִישׁ הַמֵּת שָׂם אֶל לִבּוֹ כִּי לֹא בִּמְהֵרָה יֵצֵא מִן הַבּוֹר,
וּזְמַן רַב עוֹד יְבַלֶּה בַּשְּׁכִיבָה הַמְעֻנָּה עַל הַגַּב לְלֹא נִיעַ,
אָז אָמַר, אֵיךְ יְבַלֶּה אָדָם אֶת מוֹתוֹ, מַה נּוֹתַר לוֹ
אִם לֹא לַהֲגוֹת, לַחְקֹר וּלְפַעֲנֵחַ אֶת חִידַת חַיָּיו.

כִּי טוֹבִים וְנוֹחִים הֵם חַיֵּי הַמֵּת לַהֲגוֹת הֲגִיגִים, הוּא בּוֹדֵד,
רַק מָוֶת מָשְׁבָּע, יְלָדִים וּפְקִידִים לֹא טוֹרְדִים אוֹתוֹ,
אֵבָרוֹ לֹא קוֹפֵץ וְלִבּוֹ לֹא הוֹלֵם,
וּמֹחוֹ לֹא מוּצָף בְּדַם מַרְעָל שֶׁל תַּאֲוָה,
וְהוּא לֹא חָרֵד עַל בְּרִיאוּתוֹ, וְאֵינֶנּוּ מִתְלַבֵּט
בַּקֻּשְׁיָה מֶה עָדִיף, הִתְעַמְּלוּת אוֹ שְׂחִיָּה,
וְהוּא דוֹמֶה דִּמְיוֹן-מָה לַמְשׁוֹרֵר הַשּׁוֹכֵב לְמַרְגְּלוֹת הָהָר,
מַבִּיט לַשָּׁמַיִם הַנִּגְלִים אֵלָיו מִבַּעַד לְעַנְפֵי הָעֵץ,
וּמְדַמֶּה דְּמוּיִים עַל הָהָר וְיוֹצֵק אוֹתָם בַּחֲרוּזִים,
וּפִתְאֹם נוֹפֵל עָלָיו הָהָר וְקוֹבְרוֹ תַּחְתָּיו,
וְהוּא מַמְשִׁיךְ לִשְׁכַּב בִּתְנוּחַת הַמְשׁוֹרֵר וּמַמְשִׁיךְ לְהַרְהֵר בָּהָר,
רַק הַפַּעַם לְלֹא דְּמוּיִים וּבְלִי שׁוּם חֲרוּזִים.

and became the twisted crude laugh of a good for nothing.
All the dead lie flat, laughing crudely toward heaven
as if they saw over them hope wink
like a troupe of ugly women chortling at a disco
at the bad joke of a fat man without a penny, while in their
   hearts there's bitterness.

And the dead man takes to heart the fact that he will not
   soon rise from this hole
and a long time more he'll pass in tortuous lying on his
   back without a stir
so he says, how shall a man spend his death, what remains
if not to ponder, study and resolve the riddle of his days.

For the lives of the dead are good and fit to think thoughts,
   he's solitary
a confirmed bachelor for the rest of his days, children and
   milkmen don't bother him,
his organ doesn't jump and his heart does not beat,
and his brain is not flooded with the poisoned blood of lust
and he's not worried about his health, he's not conflicted
about the puzzle of what's preferable, gymnastics or swimming,
and he bears a certain resemblance to a poet sitting at the
   foot of a mountain,
staring at the sky revealed between the tops of the trees
and drawing analogies to the mountain and casting them
   in rhyme schemes
till suddenly the mountain falls on him and buries him beneath
and he continues lying in the poet's swoon and keeps
   musing on the mountain
only this time with no analogies and no rhyme scheme.

אָז הִדְלִיק הַמֵּת אֶת פְּנַס זִכְרוֹנוֹ הַקָּלוּשׁ, הַנּוֹטֶה לִדְעֹךְ,
וְהֵאִיר אֶת פִּנּוֹת נַפְשׁוֹ הָאֲפֵלוֹת, הַמְכֻסּוֹת סַחַב מָוֶת צוֹנֵן,
לְפַשְׁפֵּשׁ אַחַר סוֹד חַיָּיו, שִׂמְחָתָם, מְצוּקָתָם וּפִשְׁרָם.
אַךְ בִּנְבֹּר הָאִישׁ הַמֵּת בְּנַפְשׁוֹ, וְנַפְשׁוֹ מָלְאָה עִתּוֹנִים,
בְּכָל מַרְתְּפֵי נַפְשׁוֹ הִתְגּוֹלְלוּ אַךְ קִרְעֵי עִתּוֹנִים,
וַעֲרֵמוֹת עִתּוֹנִים מִלְּאוּ אַף אֶת חַדְרֵי לִבּוֹ הַכְּמוּסִים.

מַה כָּלְתָה נַפְשׁוֹ שֶׁל הָאִישׁ הַמֵּת אֶל עִתּוֹן הָעֶרֶב,
דְּבַר יוֹם בְּיוֹמוֹ בִּשְׁתֵּים-עֶשְׂרֵה בַּצָּהֳרַיִם בְּעוֹד בַּחַיִּים חַיָּתוֹ,
– הוֹי כּוֹתָרוֹת דְּשֵׁנוֹת, מַדִּיפוֹת נִיחוֹחַ צְלִי בָּשָׂר וְתַבְלִינִים.
וְהוֹי אוֹתִיּוֹת פֶּטִיט מְתוּקוֹת-פְּרִיכוֹת, נִמּוֹחוֹת בַּפֶּה! –
וּבַצָּהֳרַיִם לָפַת אֶת עִתּוֹן הָעֶרֶב,
וְהֶחֱלִיקָה עָלָיו יָדוֹ גַּם לְעֵת עֶרֶב,
וְאַף לַמָּחֳרָת עוֹד מִשְׁמֵשׁ בּוֹ קְצָת,
כְּמוֹ הַמִּשְׁמוּשׁ הַמְּכַנִּי בִּבְשַׂר אֲהוּבָה מִשְּׁכְּבָר -
כָּךְ מִלְּאוּ אוֹתוֹ עִתּוֹנִים עַד לִבְלִי הוֹתֵר דָּבָר.

עוֹד בְּצָהֳרֵי יוֹם מוֹתוֹ, וּבְעוֹדֶנּוּ חַי וּמַזִּיעַ,
קָרָא הָאִישׁ, תּוֹךְ הֲסִבּוֹ לִסְעֻדָּה, הֲמוֹן יְדִיעוֹת
עַל הַמִּתְחוֹלֵל בְּפָרַס וְעַל מִשְׁפַּחַת הַשָּׁאח הַפַּרְסִי וְעַל תְּגוּבַת אֲמֶרִיקָה,
וְעַל הַיְחָסִים הַמְּעֻזָּרִים בֵּין שַׂר הָאוֹצָר לְבֵין שַׂר הַמִּסְחָר בְּאַרְצֵנוּ.
אֵלֶּה הָיוּ הַדְּבָרִים הָאַחֲרוֹנִים בָּהֶם הָגְתָה נַפְשׁוֹ
שֶׁל הָאִישׁ הַחַי בְּצָהֳרֵי יוֹם מוֹתוֹ.
הוּא לֹא הֵבִין אֵיךְ הִגִּיעַ אֵיךְ הִגִּיעַ הַשָּׁאח הַפַּרְסִי לְמָה שֶׁהִגִּיעַ,
וּבְאִי-הֲבָנָה זוֹ, אוֹתָהּ הִקְדִּישׁ לַשָּׁאח הַפַּרְסִי,
קָפַץ עָלָיו פֶּתַע רֻגְזוֹ שֶׁל הַמָּוֶת.

66

Then the dead man lights the dim lantern of his memory, that
    tends to gutter
and illumines the dark ends of his soul, that are covered in
    death's cold mosses,
to rummage after the secret of his life, its joy, sorrow and meaning.
But as the man gnaws through his soul, his soul is full of magazines,
in all the basement of his soul roll only tatters of magazines
and piles and piles of newspapers fill even the hidden chambers
    of his heart that are unknown.

How the man's soul longs for an evening paper,
his daily bread at noon while life he lived,
– oh the juicy headlines, wafting smells of meat and spices,
and oh the little typeface sweet and crisp, melting in your mouth!
And at noon he grasped the evening paper,
and his hand brushed it even at night time,
and even the next day he fondled it a bit,
like the mechanic fondling of an old lover –
so newspapers filled him till there was not room for anything else.

Even at noon on the day of his death, while still he lived in sweat,
the man read as he sat to his repast, lots of news items
about what was happening in Iran
and the family of the Shah of Iran
and about the American reaction
and about the strange dealings between
the ministers of Trade and Treasury in our fair land.
These were the last things his soul pondered
the man who lived at noon on the day of his death.
He didn't understand how the Shah of Iran
got to where he got to,
and in this confusion over the Shah of Iran
death jumped on him suddenly in all its rage.

וּבְגֶשֶׁת הָאִישׁ הַמֵּת לְפַעֲנֵחַ אֶת פֵּשֶׁר חַיָּיו,
רָאָה אֶת הַשַּׁאַח הַפַּרְסִי מֵצִיץ מִמַּרְתְּפֵי נַפְשׁוֹ
(הוּא וְאִשְׁתּוֹ וּשְׁלֹשֶׁת יְלָדָיו מָצְאוּ שָׁם מִקְלָט),
וְשַׂר הָאוֹצָר וְשַׂר הַמִּסְתָּר וְהַשַּׁדְכָנִית הַוְּתִיקָה וְנוּס כַּץ,
וְעוֹד הֲמוֹן רָאשֵׁי מֶמְשָׁלָה וְשָׂרִים וְאַלּוּפִים וְחַבְרֵי כְּנֶסֶת,
וְסַרְסוּרִים וְגַנָּבִים וְקַרְיָנֵי טֶלֶוִיזְיָה וְשַׂחֲקָנֵי כַּדּוּרֶגֶל,
הֵם וּנְשׁוֹתֵיהֶם וְטַפָּם בְּהָמוֹן רַב וָרֹעַשׁ,
וְכָל הַסַּחִי הַנִּלְוֶה אֲלֵיהֶם מִתּוֹךְ מְצוּלַת הָעִתּוֹנִים,
וְהֵם צוֹוְחִים וְרוֹקְדִים בְּמַרְתְּפֵי נַפְשׁוֹ שֶׁל הָאִישׁ הַמֵּת,
וְאוֹכְלִים וּמַפְרִישִׁים וּמִטַּנְּפִים וְיוֹרְקִים וְזָבִים,
וְתִקְרַת נַפְשׁוֹ שֶׁל הָאִישׁ הַמֵּת מְפֻיַּחַת,
מְכֻסָּה אֲדֵי הֶבֶל הָאֲנָשִׁים הַסְּמִיךְ וְעָתָם,
הָעוֹלִים בְּצַחֲנָה מִלַּהַג פִּיהֶם וּנְשִׁימַת אַפָּם,
וּמִבֵּיתֵי שֶׁחְיָם וּמֵחוֹרֵי עָרְוָתָם וּמֵרַקְבּוּבִית אֶצְבְּעוֹת רַגְלֵיהֶם,
וְרִצְפַּת נַפְשׁוֹ שֶׁל הָאִישׁ הַמֵּת מְזֹהֶמֶת
בְּרָקָם וּקְלִפּוֹתֵיהֶם וּפֵרוּרֵיהֶם וַעֲטִיפוֹתֵיהֶם הָרֵיקוֹת
שֶׁל מַאַכְלֵי הָאֲנָשִׁים וְשֶׁתֶן הַיְלָדִים הַנִּסְרָחִים אַחֲרֵיהֶם וְנִיעַ אַפָּם.

אָז יָדַע הָאִישׁ הַמֵּת כִּי רָמָה בִּידֵי הָעוֹלָם,
וְכִי אֵין לוֹ בָּסִיס וָחֹמֶר לְפַעֲנֵחַ אֶת פֵּשֶׁר חַיָּיו,
וְכִי נַפְשׁוֹ עֲצֻבָה בְּתַבְנִית בֵּית-הַכִּסֵּא הַצְּבָאִי
בּוֹ קַיָּם מַחְסוֹר נִצְחִי בִּנְיָר טוּאָלֶט,
וְעַל כֵּן מִתְגּוֹלְלִים-מֻשְׁלָכִים בּוֹ קִרְעֵי עִתּוֹנֵי הָעֶרֶב,

And when the man set to deciphering his life's meaning,
he saw the Shah of Iran peep at him from his soul's cellars
(he and his wife and his three children had applied there for
    asylum)
and the minister of Trade and Treasury and noted
    matchmaker Venus Katz,
and many more Presidents and ministers and generals and
    members of parliament
and pimps and car thieves and television presenters and
    football players,
they and their wives and their kids in a great milling multitude
with all the ordure accompanying them from the depths of
    the newspapers,
and they're squealing and parading in the cellars of the soul
    of the dead man
and eating and moving their bowels and making a mess, they
    spit and suppurate
and the ceiling of the dead man's soul is begrimed,
smeared with the vapour of these people and their sweat,
that rises in a stink from the prattle of their mouths and
    breath of their noses,
and from their armpits and holes in their loins and goop
    between their toe nails
and the floor of the dead man's soul is rank
with the spat out shells and crumbs and empty sweet
    wrappers of men
and piss of children trailing after them with noses running.

Then the man knew that he'd been cheated by the world,
and that he'd no foundation and data from which to decipher
    life's meaning
and that his soul was shaped like an army crapper
where there's an endless shortage of tissue
and so many torn ends of evening newspaper

וְכָל קֶרַע עִתּוֹן מֵכִיל בְּדַל יְדִיעָה מְקֻמָּט אוֹ כְּנַף מַאֲמָר מְעוּכָה,
וּמָרוּחַ בַּתָּוֶךְ בִּמְרִיחָה וּמִתְגּוֹלֵל עַל הָאָרֶץ לְכָל רוּחַ.

צָחַק הַשַּׂאח הַפַּרְסִי, וְשָׂחֲקוּ לְעֻמָּתוֹ יְלָדָיו,
וְצָחֲקוּ שָׂרֵי הָאוֹצָר וְהַמִּסְחָר (כָּל אֶחָד לְחוּד),
וְצָחֲקָה וָנוֹס כֵּן, וְהִיא כְּבָר מְזֻוֶּגֶת אִישׁ צוֹחֵק לְאִשָּׁה מִתְפַּקַּעַת,
וּסְבִיבָם הָמוֹן צוֹחֵק צְוֹחַל וְחוֹגֵג.

וְהָאִישׁ הַמֵּת צָעַק צְעָקָה אֲנוּשָׁה עַל חַיָּיו הַמְּאוּסִים שֶׁאָבְדוּ,
וְאִישׁ לֹא שָׁמַע אֶת שַׁוְעַת הַמֵּת הָאַיֹּמָה
כִּי הָיְתָה חֲנוּקָה בַּחֲלַל לְעוֹ הַמָּלֵא וְדָחוּס אֲדָמָה.

וְקוֹל לֹא נִשְׁמַע בַּקֶּבֶר, וְהָיְתָה דְמָמָה,
זוּלַת קוֹל תְּסִיסָה קַל, קוֹל לַחַשׁ סוֹד,
כְּקוֹל נְפִיחַת אֲחוֹרַיִם חֲרִישִׁית,
כְּקוֹל הֶחָלִיל הַמְנַגֵּן כֹּה חֵרֵשׁ
עַד כִּי נִשְׁמַעַת בּוֹ רַק נְשִׁימַת פִּי הַמְחַלֵּל,
הֲלֹא הוּא קוֹל הַגּוּף הַמַּרְקִיב בְּעֶצֶב,
מֵפִיק צְלִילִים רוֹמַנְטִיִּים נוּגִים.

וְהָאִישׁ הַמֵּת הַצַּג כִּכְלִי רֵיק,
וְחִידַת חַיָּיו הַמְּאוּסִים
הָיְתָה לְמִדְרַךְ סוּלְיוֹת נַעֲלֵיהֶם
שֶׁל בְּנֵי מִשְׁפַּחַת הַשַּׂאח הַפַּרְסִי,

וּשְׂפָתָיו לוֹאֲטוֹת בְּחִיּוּךְ מִתְחַנֵּף
אֶת מְחִיר הַדּוֹלָר וּמְחִיר הַנֵּפְט.

70

roll there and every tear of newspaper
contains a tail end of crumpled news or squished story
and is wiped in the middle with a good wipe and rolls on the
    earth to where it will.

The Shah of Iran laughed, and his children laughed in turn
and the minister of Trade and Treasury laughed (one by one),
and Venus Katz laughed, and she's already pairing up a
    laughing man
with a woman busting a gut,
and around them a multitude laughs and cheers and celebrates.

And the dead man cried a desperate cry for his base life that
    was lost,
and no one heard the dead man's awful moan
for it was choked in the hollow of his mouth that was stuffed
    with earth.

And not a sound was heard at the graveside, and there was silence
except for a little simmering, a whispering hiss,
like the sound of a silent fart,
like the sound of a flute that plays so quiet,
till all that's heard is the flautist's breath
which is the voice of the body that's sadly rotting
and makes such a sad romantic noise.

And the dead man was shown as an empty vessel
and the riddle of his base life
was a foot pad for the soles of the shoes
of the relations of the Shah of Iran.

And his lips lap with an obsequious grin
the exchange rate of the dollar and price of kerosene.

71

פרק שלישי

וְעוֹד תְּשׁוּקָה נוֹתְרָה לוֹ לַמֵּת,
לְהֵאָסֵף אֶל חֵיק אָבִיו,
לִטְמֹן אֶת פָּנָיו הַמִּתְפּוֹרְרִים
וְלִבְכּוֹת בְּצַוַּאר מוֹלִידוֹ הַמַּרְקִיב.

וְעָנְתָה לוֹ גֻּלְגֹּלֶת הָאָב הַצּוֹחֵק:
גַּם לִי הָיָה אַבָּא וְגַם לִי מִתְחַשֵּׁק.

אַט אַט נִמְחוּ תָּוֵי פָּנָיו שֶׁל הָאִישׁ הַמֵּת,
צוּרַת גּוּפוֹ הָלְכָה וְצָמְצְמָה,
הַטֶּבַע סָתַם אֶת הָאִישׁ הַמֵּת לִהְיוֹת מְעֻצָּב
בְּתַבְנִיתָם הָאֲחִידָה שֶׁל כָּל הַמֵּתִים הַקּוֹדְמִים לוֹ.

וּמִסְגֶּרֶת מוֹתָר שְׂפָתָיו הִתְלַכְּדָה עִם הֶעָפָר
וְנִטְמְעָה בְּתוֹךְ הָאֲדָמָה הַמַּקִּיפָה אוֹתָהּ,
וְחִיּוּכוֹ הַנִּכְלָם שֶׁל הָאִישׁ הַמֵּת הָלַךְ וְהִטַּשְׁטֵשׁ
וְנָמוֹג בְּמַעֲבֶה הָאֲדָמָה.

וְהָאִישׁ הַמֵּת שָׁכַח אֶת קְלוֹנוֹ וְשָׁכַח אֶת הַשֵּׂאת הַפַּרְסִי
וְאֶת שַׂר הָאוֹצָר וְאֶת שַׂר הַמִּסְתָּר וְאֶת הַשַּׁדְכָנִית וְנוּס כַּץ,
וְכָל קַרְעֵי עִתּוֹנֵי הָעֶרֶב הָיוּ לְעִסָּה דְּבִיקָה
וְהִתְעָרְבְּבוּ בְּאַשְׁפַּת הַיְּקוּם הַכְּלָלִית,
וְהַמֵּת שֶׁזָּעַק עִם רִדְתּוֹ אֶל הַבּוֹר וּבָכָה יָמִים רַבִּים
כְּבָר הָיָה שָׁקֵט עַכְשָׁו, מָסוּר וְנֶאֱמָן לְתַהֲלִיךְ מוֹתוֹ,
תַּלְמִיד שַׁקְדָן שֶׁל טֶבַע הַהִתְפּוֹרְרוּת וְהַכְּלָיָה,
נָקִי וְחַף מִכֹּל מַגָּע עִם הַחַיִּים אֲשֶׁר לְמַעְלָה,
צַדִּיק פָּרוּשׁ, נָזִיר שַׁתְקָן, טוֹבֵל בְּדִמְמַת מוֹתוֹ,
וְגַבִּינָיו מוּרָמִים מְעַט בַּאֲרֶשֶׁת הִתְחַסְּדוּת נַעֲלָה.

CHAPTER THREE

And one more desire the dead man had left
to be taken to his father's bosom
and hide his crumbling face
and weep with his arms round the neck
of his progenitor that's rotting.

And the laughing gold skull of his father refrained:
I too had a father and I too yearned.

Slowly, slowly the lines of the dead man's face vanished,
the shape of his body gradually shrank,
nature carved the dead man to the style
and single mould of all the dead from way back.

And the remaining frame of his lips locked with the dust
and hid in the earth surrounding it
and the shamed smile of the man gradually dimmed
and melted in the thick of the earth.

And the dead man forgot his ignominy and forgot the Shah of Iran
and the minister of Trade and Treasury and the matchmaker
    Venus Katz,
and all the ends of evening newspaper became a sticky paste
and mixed with the universe's general rubbish
and the dead man who cried as he was lowered in the hole
    and wept for many days
was already quiet now, faithfully devoted to the process
    of his death,
a dedicated student of the nature of decomposition and the kidney,
innocent and untouched by any contact with the life over his head,
a retired righteous man, silent monk,
purifying in the silence of his death,
and his brows raised a little in an expression of spiritual uplift.

וּבְשֶׁקַע כָּל זַהֲמַת חַיָּיו, וּבְהִצְטַלֵּל עָלָיו נַפְשׁוֹ,
הִקְשִׁיב הָאִישׁ הַמֵּת אֶל תּוֹכוֹ,
וְהָיְתָה דְמָמָה, שְׁלֵמָה וּמֻחְלֶטֶת הָיְתָה הַדְּמָמָה,
וּבְאֶמְצַע הַשֶּׁקֶט, בְּלֵב הַדּוּמִיָּה, כְּמוֹ סִירָה עַל חֶלְקַת מַיִם קְרוּשִׁים,
שָׁמַע הֲמִיָּה חֲרִישִׁית דַּקָּה, הֲמִיַּת יֶלֶד קָטָן,
מִין צִפְצוּף שֶׁהָיָה מְקֻפָּל וְצָפוּף בְּתוֹכְכֵי נַפְשׁוֹ
שָׁנִים כֹּה רַבּוֹת, כְּמוֹ שֶׁמְּקֻפָּל הַצִּיּוּץ הָרִאשׁוֹן
בַּחֲזֵה הַגּוֹזָל הַטָּמוּן בַּבֵּיצָה,
הֲלֹא הִיא הַהֲמִיָּה הַנִּצְחִית, הַלֹּא נִדְלֵית וְהַלֹּא מִתְמַצֵּית,
הֲמִיַּת הַיֶּלֶד לִהְיוֹת תָּלוּי עַל צַוְּאר אָבִיו.

כִּי מָה עוֹד נִשְׁאַר בָּנוּ בְּהִתְקַלֵּף מֵעָלֵינוּ
הָעִתּוֹן וְהָאִשָּׁה וּמְעַט הַפַּרְנָסָה? –
הַהִנָּשְׂאוּת לְמַעְלָה בִּזְרוֹעוֹת אָבִינוּ, כְּבִישַׁת הַפָּנִים הַחֲרֵדוֹת
בֵּין בְּשַׂר צַוָּארוֹ הַחַם הַנּוֹדֵף רֵיחַ סַבּוֹן רַעֲנָן
לְבֵין צַוְּארוֹן חֻלְצָתוֹ הַמְגֹהָץ.

שָׁם, בַּמָּקוֹם הַזֶּה, חֶלְקָה יָדַעְנוּ, שֶׁקְּעַרוּרִית חַמָּה
בֵּין הַצַּוָּאר לַשֶּׁכֶם, אִי קָטָן שֶׁל תַּנְחוּמֵי מַרְגּוֹעַ.
הָאִי הַזֶּה אָבַד, אֲבָל עוֹדֶנּוּ מְחַפְּשִׂים בְּכָל אָדָם
אֶת הַזְּרוֹעוֹת שֶׁיִּשָּׂאוּנוּ מַעְלָה,
בְּכָל פָּנִים – אֶת נַהֲרַת אָבִינוּ הָרוֹחֵץ
בְּטַל שֶׁל אַהֲבָה אֶת דִּמְעוֹתֵינוּ.

כָּל הָאֲנָשִׁים, בֵּין בְּנֵי שָׁנָה, בֵּין בְּנֵי שִׁבְעִים,
בֵּין חַיִּים וּבֵין מֵתִים, זְקוּקִים לְאַבָּא.

הִנֵּה הַזּוֹנָה הָעוֹמֶדֶת בְּקֶרֶן הָרְחוֹב לְעֵת עֶרֶב,
וְהִנֵּה הָאִישׁ הַזָּקֵן הַנִּגָּשׁ אֵלֶיהָ.
הִיא יְתוֹמָה. אָמְנָם יֵשׁ לָהּ שָׁדַיִם וִירֵכַיִם,
וְלִכְאוֹרָה מַה נָּחוּץ לָהּ יוֹתֵר, וּבְכָל זֹאת
עֵינֶיהָ מִתְרוֹצְצוֹת, בָּרוּר: אֵין לָהּ אַבָּא.

And with the sinking of his life's filth and clarification of his soul,
the dead man listened to his innards
and there was silence, complete and absolute was the silence,
and in the middle of the quiet, the heart of stillness, like a boat
on a section of congealed lake water,
he heard a faint silent keen, the keen of a little boy,
a kind of peep that was folded and cramped in the inmost
    part of his soul
so many years, like the first cheep crushed
in the breast of the chick hidden in the egg,
for is it not the eternal keen, that is not drawn and is not drained,
the keen of the boy to be hung upon the neck of his Dad.

For what more is left in us when we peel away –
the paper and the wife and a crust of bread?
Being held up in our father's arms, the frightened face pressed
in between hot neck, smelling of fresh soap
and the collar of his fresh pressed shirt.

There, in that place, a spot we've known, a warm hollow
between the neck and armpit, a little island of tranquillity.
This island is lost, but we still search in every person
for arms that will lift us up,
in every face – the glow of our father that floods
with love's dew our tears.

All of the people, from one year old to seventy
whether alive or dead, all need Daddy.

Here's the hooker standing on the corner at nightfall
and here's the old man going up to her.
She's an orphan. Though she has breasts and thighs,
and apparently something more useful, still
her eyes dart around, clearly: she has no Daddy.

וְהָאִישׁ הַזָּקֵן, מֵאֵלָיו מוּבָן, גַּם הוּא יָתוֹם.
וּשְׁנֵי הַיְתוֹמִים נִפְגָּשִׁים, שְׁנֵיהֶם חֲרֵדִים מְעַט,
הֵם מִשְׁתּוִּים בַּמֶּחִיר, הֵם נִכְנָסִים לָחָצֵר,
הוּא מַפְשִׁיל מִכְנָסַיִם וְהִיא – שִׂמְלָה,
וְזַכְרוּת יְתוֹמָה מִתְרוֹמֶמֶת-נוֹפֶלֶת -
אִי זְרוֹעוֹתָיו הַתּוֹמְכוֹת שֶׁל אַבָּא! -
וְנִפְשָׁקֶת מוּלָהּ עֶרְוָה יְתוֹמָה, וְעוֹד רֶגַע,
וְצַעַר גָּדוֹל שֶׁל יַתְמוּת אוֹפֵף
תְּרֵיסַר (אוֹ פָּחוֹת) תְּנוּעוֹת רְפוּיוֹת
כְּבַקְדִּישׁ יָתוֹם בְּבֹקֶר טֵבֶת,
בְּעוֹד שׁוֹטֵר יָתוֹם מִתְגַּנֵּב אֶל הֶחָצֵר
וְתוֹפֵס אֶת שְׁנֵי הַיְתוֹמִים בְּעָרְפָּם
וּמוֹבִיל אוֹתָם אֶל מְכוֹנִית הַמִּשְׁטָרָה,
שָׁם הֵם יוֹשְׁבִים, מְכֻנָּסִים, שְׁלָשְׁתָּם,
שְׁלֹשָׁה יְתוֹמִים בִּשְׁתִיקָה מוּעָקְתָּם,
בְּלִי דַעַת עַל מָה וְאֵיךְ וּמַדּוּעַ,
וְצוֹפַר מְכוֹנִית הַמִּשְׁטָרָה מְיַלֵּל בִּנְהִי-בְּכִי גָּדוֹל:
כָּאן נוֹסְעִים שְׁלֹשָׁה אֲנָשִׁים שֶׁאִבְּדוּ אֶת אַבָּא.

וְהָאִישׁ הַמֵּת שָׁכַב עַל מִשְׁכָּבוֹ, וְתַבְנִית הַשֶּׁלֶד
כְּבָר מִצְטַיֶּרֶת מִבַּעַד לִקְרָעֵי בְּשָׂרוֹ הַנּוֹתָרִים,
וּפָנָיו מוּסַבִּים אֶל עַל, קְשׁוּבִים, וְחִכָּה לְאָבִיו.

וּבְאַהֲבָתְךָ אֲנִי בוֹטֵחַ, אָבִי, וַאֲנִי יוֹדֵעַ
כִּי בּוֹא תָּבוֹא בְּקָרְאִי אֵלֶיךָ. וּכְפִי שֶׁאֲנִי בוֹטֵחַ בַּמָּוֶת
אֲנִי יוֹדֵעַ כִּי יָבוֹא, עוֹד יוֹתֵר
אֲנִי בוֹטֵחַ בְּאָבִי, כִּי מִי זֶה
אִם לֹא אָבִי הָעוֹמֵד שָׁם מֵאֲחוֹרֵי שַׁעַר הַמָּוֶת,
וּבְיָדוֹ הָאַחַת מִזְוָדָה בָּהּ צְרוּרִים בְּגָדֵי קַיִץ שֶׁלִּי, בֶּגֶד-יָם וּמַגֶּבֶת,
וּבְיָדוֹ הַשְּׁנִיָּה תִּיק אֹכֶל, וּבוֹ לַחְמָנִיָּה בְּחֶמְאָה וַאֲפַרְסֵק,

And the old man, it goes without saying, he too is orphaned.
And two orphans meet, both a little scared,
they fix a price, they go in the yard,
he drops his pants and she – her dress,
and an orphan manhood rises – falls –
where are the uplifting arms of Daddy!
– and spread before it an orphan crotch and in another minute,
the great sorrow of orphan-hood enfolds
a dozen (or fewer) feeble thrusts
like an orphan's kaddish on a morning of Tevet,
and as an orphan cop sneaks in the yard
and catches the two orphans by the neck
and leads them to the patrol car
there they sit, an enclosed trio,
three orphans in the silence of their ache,
without knowing what and where and how,
and the paddy wagon's siren wails out the great sob:
here ride three people that lost their Daddy.

And the dead man lay on his couch, and the mould of a skeleton
was already drawn through the torn ends of his flesh,
and his face is turned on high, expectantly, and waits for
    his Daddy.

In your love I trust, Daddy, I know
that you will come when I call. And as I trust in death
and know he'll come, all the more
I trust my Daddy, for who
if not my Daddy stands behind the gate of death
and in his hand a suitcase holding all my summer clothes,
swimming trunks and towel,
and in his other hand a lunch basket, and in it a buttered
    roll and pear

וּבַתָּוֶךְ נִצָּב הוּא, אָבִי, מְחַכֶּה לִי וּמְחַיֵּךְ:
מַה, לֹא יָדַעְתָּ שֶׁמֵּעֵבֶר לַמָּוֶת יֵשׁ קַיְטָנָה,
וֵאלֹהִים הוּא הַמַּצִּיל?

וּבְעִיר אַחֶרֶת, בְּבֵית קְבָרוֹת אַחֵר, יָשֵׁן,
שָׁכַב אָבִיו שֶׁל הָאִישׁ הַמֵּת, וְהוּא שֶׁלֶד גָּמוּר,
דַּיָּר וָתִיק בָּעוֹלָם הַנָּוּוּל וְהַבֹּשֶׁת,
וּמִתּוֹךְ גֻּלְגָּלְתּוֹ הַחֲשׂוּפָה קוֹרֵן חִיּוּךְ זְוָעָה.

הֵן גַּם הוּא, הָאַבָּא, יָתוֹם הוּא, וְגַם לוֹ יֵשׁ אַבָּא,
וְגַם הוּא רוֹצֶה, לָמָּה לֹא, לְהָלִיט פָּנָיו בְּצַוַּאר אָבִיו
וְלִמְצֹא תַּנְחוּמֵי עוֹלָם לְחַיָּיו וּמוֹתוֹ.

וְגַם לְאָבִיו שֶׁל אַבָּא יֵשׁ אַבָּא.
וְכָל הָאָבוֹת הֵם בָּנִים, וּבְהִתְקַלֵּף מֵעֲלֵיהֶם קְלִפַּת עוֹרָם
וְהִנֵּה יְלָדִים הֵם, כֻּלָּם חוֹלְמִים לְהִנָּשֵׂא לְמַעְלָה
אֶל בְּשַׂר צַוָּארוֹ הָרָחוּץ בְּסַבּוֹן רַעֲנָן שֶׁל אַבָּא.

הוֹי מֵתִים עֲלוּבִים, מַה תַּעֲשׂוּ אִם תֵּצְאוּ מִן הַקֶּבֶר,
תְּטַפְּסוּ זֶה עַל זֶה, יָתוֹם עַל אָבִיו,
וְתִצְּרוּ שַׁרְשֶׁרֶת שֶׁלָּדִים מְגֻחֶכֶת, סֻלָּם עֲצָמוֹת
שֶׁל אָבוֹת וּבָנִים שֶׁרֹאשׁוֹ נֶעֱלָם בַּשָּׁמַיִם?
וְאֵיךְ תְּנַחֲמוּ זֶה אֶת זֶה, כִּי כַּאֲשֶׁר יִתָּלֶה הָאָב
בִּשְׁתֵּי יָדָיו בְּצַוַּאר אָבִיו, אֵיךְ יֹאחַז אֶת בְּנוֹ?

מִי יְנַחֵם אֶת מִי? מִי יִשְׁכַּב בְּחֵיק מִי? הֲמוֹן פְּגָרִים
רְעֵבֵי תַּנְחוּמִים יָרִיבוּ עַל חֵיק?
וְאֵיפֹה הַחֵיק? אֵיפֹה בְּשַׂר הַצַּוָּאר? מִי הֵרִיחַ פֹּה
פַּעַם רֵיחַ סַבּוֹן רַעֲנָן?

הוֹי מֵתִים עֲלוּבִים, כָּאן לֹא קָלִיפוֹרְנְיָה,
כָּאן קֶבֶר חָשׁוּךְ וְזֶהוּ הַמָּוֶת!
עַל כֵּן יַעֲזָב בֵּן אֶת אָבִיו וְאִמּוֹ
וְאִישׁ אֶת אִשְׁתּוֹ וְדָבַק בְּמוֹתוֹ.

78

and in the breach he stands, my Dad, and waits for me and smiles:
What, didn't you know that after death there is a summer camp
and God is the life guard?

And in another town, in another graveyard, old
lay the Daddy of the dead man, all skeleton
a veteran resident of the world of carrion and shame
and from his exposed skull beams a horrified grin.

For he too, the Daddy, is an orphan too, he too has no Daddy,
and he too wants, why not, to hide his face in his father's neck
and find there the consolations of his life and death.

And his father too has a Daddy, a Daddy.
And all the fathers are sons, and when you peel back their skins
and see they're little children, and all dream of being raised up
to the soap washed fresh neck flesh of Daddy.

Oh miserable dead, what will you do if you exit your graves,
climb one over another, orphan over his sire,
and form a motley chain of skeletons, a ladder of bones,
of sons and fathers whose head will disappear into the clouds?
And how will you console one another, for when the father hangs
his two hands on his father's throat, how will he handle his son?

Who will console whom? Who lie in the bosom of whom? Many
consolation hungry stiffs will quarrel over a bosom?
And where is the bosom? Where is the neck? Did anybody ever
    catch a whiff
here even once of the smell of fresh soap?

Oh miserable dead, this isn't California,
this is the dark grave and this is death!
So shall a son leave his father and mother
and man leave his wife and cleave unto his death.

79

וְהָאִישׁ הַמֵּת רָאָה אֵיךְ בּוֹגֵד בּוֹ אָבִיו.
וְגִלְגֵּל אָבִיו חִזְּקָה אֶת חִיּוּךְ הַזְּוָעָה שֶׁלָּהּ.
וְחִזְּקָה עִמָּהּ גַּלְגֻּלֵת אָבִיו שֶׁל הָאָב, וְחִזְּכוּ
אֲבוֹת אֲבוֹתָיו עַד סוֹף כָּל הַדּוֹרוֹת.
וּכְמוֹ שֶׁמַּבְהִיק חִיּוּךְ הַקָּהָל בְּחֶשְׁכַת אוּלַם הַתֵּיאַטְרוֹן
לְמַרְאֵה קוֹמֶדְיָה בָּלָה (לֹא חִיּוּךְ שֶׁל עֹנֶג,
רַק חִיּוּךְ שֶׁל שִׂמְחָה-לְאֵיד לְקִלּוֹן הַשַּׂחְקָנִים מְבַזֵּי-עַצְמָם),
כָּךְ, מִתּוֹךְ אֲפֵלַת מַרְתְּפֵי קִבְרֵיהֶם, זָרְחוּ חִיּוּכֵי הַזְּוָעָה,
וְגֻלְגָּלוֹת מִתְגַּלְגְּלוֹת בִּצְחוֹק-חֶרֶשׁ
לְמַרְאֵה מוֹת הַבֵּן הַנִּצְחִי, תִּקְוָתוֹ הַנּוֹאֶלֶת לְהֵאָסֵף אֶל חֵיק אָבִיו,
וְזַעֲקָתוֹ הַמָּרָה בַּבּוֹר, זוֹ הַזְּעָקָה הַנִּצְחִית, הַמִּתְגַּלְגֶּלֶת אֵינְסוֹפִית,
וּמַרְנִינָה, אִישׁ בְּתוֹרוֹ, אֶת קָהַל שׁוֹכְנֵי הַבּוֹר.

עִם הַמָּוֶת מַתָּרִים קִשְׁרֵי הַמִּשְׁפָּחָה,
וּבֵן לְאָבִיו כְּכֶלֶב,
וּבְלֵיל הַסֵּדֶר אִישׁ לְעַצְמוֹ
עַצְמוֹתָיו יְלַקֵּק בִּבְדִידוּת מְנֻעֶלֶת.

אָבִינוּ, אֲשֶׁר אוֹתָנוּ אָהַב,
פִּיו פָּעוּר לַשָּׁמַיִם: הַב הַב!

And the dead man saw how his father betrayed him.
And his father's skull grinned its horrified grin.
And with it grinned his father's father's skull, and grinned
his fathers' fathers to the last generation.
And as the audience's smile gleams in the dark of an auditorium
at seeing the threadbare comedy (not a smile of pleasure,
but a smile of delight at the misery of actors embarrassing
   themselves)
so, from the darkness of their cellar graves, shone the
   horrified grins
and skulls upon skulls upon skulls rolled in silent mirth
at the sight of the eternal son, his foolish hope to be taken to
   his father's bosom,
and his bitter cry in the hole, this is the eternal cry, that
   rolls endlessly
gladdens the heart, each in his turn, of the audience of
   hole residents.

With death the bonds of family are loosed
and son to his father's a dog
and on Passover night each one by one
will lick his own bones alone.
Our father, who us did love,
his mouth is gaped to heaven: ruff, ruff!

81

פרק רביעי

וְהָאִישׁ הַמֵּת חָלָה מֵרֹב צַעַר,
וּבְשָׂרוֹ נַעֲשָׂה רָזֶה,
וּשְׂפָתָיו הַחֲוֵרוֹת נֶאֶכְלוּ מֵעַל פִּיו,
וְשִׁנָּיו נֶחְשְׂפוּ בְּחִיּוּךְ נִבְזֶה.

וְהָאִישׁ קָרַע מִפָּנָיו אֶת הַחִיּוּךְ,
וְהִנֵּה מִתַּחְתָּיו צָץ גִּחוּךְ.

עִם כְּלוֹת הַבָּשָׂר הוֹבִישׁוּ מִשְׁאֲלוֹת הַלֵּב.
הַחַיִּים, הַחֲלוֹמוֹת הֵם בַּבָּשָׂר. עַכְשָׁו
כָּלָה בָּשָׂר. מִי בַּתּוֹר? הָעֶצֶם.

לְלֹא בְּכִי וָצַעַר וּלְלֹא נִפְנוּפֵי מִטְפַּחַת
נִפְרְדוּ עַצְמוֹת הָאִישׁ הַמֵּת מִן הַגּוּף הָאֶחָד
וְהָלְכוּ, עֶצֶם עֶצֶם לְדַרְכָּהּ.
כְּמוֹ שֶׁנִּתָּקוֹת הַזְּעָקוֹת מִפִּי הַזּוֹעֵק,
נִתָּקוֹת מִן הַכְּאֵב אֲשֶׁר הוֹלִיד אוֹתָן,
וְיוֹצְאוֹת לָשׁוּט בָּאֲוִיר, בְּנוֹת קוֹל מְפֻזָּזוֹת,
כָּךְ פָּרְשׁוּ עַצְמוֹת הַגּוּף מִן הָאִישׁ הַמֵּת
לְהִתְגּוֹלֵל הִתְגּוֹלְלוּת עַצְמָאִית בֶּעָפָר.

וְהָאִישׁ הַמֵּת הָלַךְ וְקָטֹן, וְהָלַךְ וְצָמַק,
קְטָעִים קְטָעִים נִכְחֲדוּ מִמֶּנּוּ.
הָרֶגֶל נִתְּקָה מִן הַגּוּף וּפָרְשָׁה
וְהָיְתָה לְעֶבְדָּה נִפְרֶדֶת,
פָּרְשׁוּ הַיָּדַיִם זוֹ מִזּוֹ וְהָיוּ לְזָרוֹת,
מַה לִּי וָלָךְ, הָיִינוּ אַחָיוֹת,
מָחָאנוּ כַּפַּיִם, עַכְשָׁו הַזְּדַקֵּנּוּ,
שְׁתֵּי רְוָקוֹת אֲפֹרוֹת, קְשׁוּחוֹת,
לְהִתְפּוֹרֵר יוֹדְעוֹת אֲנַחְנוּ לְבַד.

אָכֵן, רִקְמַת הָעֶצֶם הִיא קָשׁוּחָה, לֹא תָּמֵס אוֹתָהּ
בְּגַעְגּוּעִים וְזִכְרוֹנוֹת; עוֹלָם אַחֵר, קָשֶׁה זָר
אֶצְלֵנוּ מִסְתַּתֵּר מִתַּחַת לַבָּשָׂר; הָעֶצֶם לֹא אוֹהֶבֶת,

82

CHAPTER FOUR

And the dead man was sick with sorrow
and his flesh wasted away
and his pale lips ate back from his mouth
and his teeth were bared in a base grin.

And the man tore from his face the grin
and there underneath it rose a chortling.

With the flesh gone the heart's desire dried.
Life, dreams are of flesh. Now
flesh was gone. Who's next in line? The bone.

Without tears and sorrow and without waving a hanky
bones took their leave of the dead man, from the one body
and left, each bone on its solitary way.
As cries lose touch with the crier's mouth,
lose touch with the pain that gave them birth,
and set sail in the air, playful gusts of sound,
so the bones quit the body of the dead man
to roll an independent roll through the ground.

And the dead man continually shrank, and continually shrivelled,
bit by bit of him was lost.
The leg detached from the body and went its way
and became a separate entity.
The hands left one another and became estranged,
what are you to me, we were sisters,
we clapped together, now we're grown old,
two grey spinsters, hard bitten,
falling apart is something we can manage to do alone.

Indeed, the mesh of bone is tough, you will not melt it
with longings and memories; another world, hard and strange
hides beneath our flesh; bone does not love

לֹא זוֹכֶרֶת, לֹא נָשִׁים וְלֹא אוֹר שֶׁמֶשׁ, בְּקוֹל שֶׁפְּשׁוּף,
כְּמוֹ קוֹל גֵּרוּד הַחֶרֶס, מִתְפּוֹרֶרֶת, וּבְנַקִּישַׁת הָעֶצֶם הַנִּשְׁבֶּרֶת
מִתְרַחֵק-נִשְׁכָּח צִבְיוֹן הַגּוּף הַחַי.

שָׁלוֹם רַגְלַי, שָׁלוֹם יָדַי, שָׁלוֹם אַגָּן יְרֵכַי וְצַלְעוֹתַי,
שָׁלוֹם שִׁדְרָה וְחֻלְיוֹת הַצַּוָּאר, שָׁלוֹם לְכֻלְּכֶם,
יָדַעְנוּ יַחַד מִין מִבְנֵה רוֹפֵף שֶׁל כֹּחַ סֵבֶל
שֶׁנִּשָּׂא עָלָיו בַּאֲנָחָה שַׂק מָלֵא נְתָחֵי בָשָׂר
לִכְבוֹד הֶחָג, הֶחָג עָבַר, כַּרְסֵם לוֹ הַבָּשָׂר,
הִגִּיעָה עֵת לְהִפָּרֵד גַּם מִן הָעֶצֶם הַנּוֹשֵׂאת,
הֵן עוֹנַת פְּרִידוֹת לָנוּ עַכְשָׁו, עֲלֵי הָעֵץ
נוֹשְׁרִים בַּסְּתָו, כָּךְ מְאַבֵּד גּוּפֵנוּ אֶת עָלָיו.

וּמִן הָאִישׁ הַמֵּת נוֹתָר אַךְ כַּדּוּר הַגֻּלְגֹּלֶת הַקָּטֹן,
וּבוֹ אַרְבָּעָה חוֹרִים סְתוּמִים וּפְקוּקִים בָּאֲדָמָה,
וְכֵיוָן שֶׁבְּשַׂר הַשְּׂפָתַיִם נֶאֱכַל כֻּלּוֹ וְשִׁנָּיו נֶחְשְׂפוּ עַד תֹּם,
אָבַד חִיּוּכוֹ הַנִּכְלָם שֶׁל הָאִישׁ הַמֵּת וְהִתְמַזֵּג בָּאֲדָמָה,
וּמִבֵּין הַלְּסָתוֹת הַחֲשׂוּפוֹת, כְּמוֹ מֵעֵצֶם שָׁבוּר, לְבַלֵּב הַחִיּוּךְ הָאַחֲרוֹן,
הֲלֹא הוּא חִיּוּךְ הַזְּוָעָה שֶׁל גֻּלְגֹּלֶת הַמֵּת.

שָׁכַב הָאִישׁ הַמֵּת בַּאֲפֵלַת קִבְרוֹ וְחִיֵּךְ אֶת חִיּוּךְ הַזְּוָעָה
אֲשֶׁר חִיְּכוּ לִקְרָאתוֹ כָּל אֲבוֹתָיו (וְהוּא מְצֹטָרֵף
אֶל קְהַל הַצּוֹפִים הַמֵּתִים, וּמְצֻפֶּה כְּבָר בְּקֹצֶר-רוּחַ
לַחֲזֹיוֹן הַמַּצְחִיק שֶׁל מוֹת בְּנוֹ, נְפִילָתוֹ אֶל הַקֶּבֶר,
וּתְשׁוּקָתוֹ הַמְגֻחֶכֶת לְהֵאָסֵף אֶל חֵיק אָבִיו).
וְשָׁכְבוּ כֻּלָּם, שָׂדֶה זָרוּעַ כַּדּוּרֵי גֻּלְגְּלָאוֹת,
אִישׁ אִישׁ כַּדּוּר גֻּלְגֹּלֶת עִוֵּר וְסָתוּם,
מְהֻדָּק בָּאֲדָמָה וְנִשְׁקָף כְּלַפֵּי מַעְלָה, אֶל רְקִיעַ הַלַּיְלָה.

does not remember, not women
and not the light of the sun, with a rubbing sound
like the sound of porcelain scratching,
it crumbles and with the knock of breaking bones
the living form recedes and is forgotten.

Goodbye legs, goodbye hands, goodbye hip sockets and spare ribs,
goodbye spine and collar bone, goodbye all of you
we knew together a kind of rickety ensemble good for taking pains
that bore on it with a sigh a sack-full of hanks of meat
for Christmas; Christmas is past, the meat consumed
it's time to part even from the bone that bears,
so now is our parting season, the tree's leaves
fall in autumn, so our body loses its leaves.

And of the dead man just a little ball of skull is left,
and in it four holes packed and bunged with earth
and since the flesh of lips is all eaten and his teeth bared to the end,
the shameful smile of the dead man is lost and he's mixed
     with the earth,
and from between bared jaws, as from a broken urn, a last
     grin blossoms
for is it not a horrified grin, in the skull of death.

The dead man lay in his grave's darkness and smiled his
     horrified grin
that all his forefathers grinned at him (and he joined in
watching the crowd of the dead, and waits expectantly
for the funny spectacle of his son's death, his fall into the grave
and his ridiculous desire to be taken to his father's bosom),
and they all lay, a field strewn with skulls,
each man a skull deaf and dumb
fastened into the earth and gazing up into the night sky.

וּמוּל רְקִיעַ הַלַּיְלָה הַמְשֻׁבָּץ כּוֹכָבִים נוֹהֲרִים -
רוֹמְזִים אֶל תִּפְאֶרֶת הַיְקוּם וְסוֹדוֹ,
יֵשׁ רָקִיעַ תַּחְתּוֹן, מְגֻלְגָּל גַּלְגַּלּוֹת צוֹחֲקוֹת -
רוֹמְזוֹת אֶל נוֹרְאוֹת הַמָּוֶת וְאֵימָתוֹ.

וְרָקִיעַ נִבָּט אֶל רָקִיעַ, כְּמוֹ בָּבוּאָה מְעֻוֶּתֶת.
וְאִישׁ כָּפוּף, הַהוֹלֵךְ יְחִידִי בַּלַּיְלָה,
מְחַפֵּשׂ רְאִי הוֹלֵם לְנֵטֶל חַיָּיו,
לֹא יִשָּׂא אֶת רֹאשׁוֹ לְמַעְלָה
וְלֹא יִשְׁתָּאֶה אֶל חִידוֹת הַיְקוּם,
רַק לְמַטָּה יַבִּיט, כִּי שָׁם הַשָּׁמַיִם הַיָּאִים לוֹ,
וְאֵין בָּהֶם סוֹד, רַק כְּאֵב נוֹקֵב,
וְאֵין בָּם חִידָה, רַק פִּתְרוֹן מְגֻנֶּה,
וְאֵין כִּפַּת תְּכֵלֶת, רַק קְלִפָּה שֶׁל לַעַג
שָׁם רִבּוֹא רִבְבָאוֹת חִיּוּכֵי זַוְעָה
זוֹרְחִים בּוֹהֲקִים מֵרְקִיעַ תַּחְתּוֹן,
כְּמוֹ כִתְמֵי שֻׁמָּן מִסְנַּר חֲנֻנִים מְזֹהָם.

אָכֵן, דּוֹמֶה הָיָה כִּי לַכְּלִימָה אֵין קֵץ,
כְּמוֹ הֵמִית הַמָּוֶת אֶת הַכֹּל
וְרַק הוֹתִיר אֶת הָעֶלְבּוֹן הַמְפַרְכֵּס.
וּכְכָל שֶׁנַּעֲשָׂה חָשׁוּךְ יוֹתֵר, וְהָיָה שָׁם חֹשֶׁךְ
לִפְנִים מֵחֹשֶׁךְ, וּכְכָל שֶׁמֵּת הָאִישׁ הַמֵּת יוֹתֵר,
וְהָלַךְ וּפָחַת וְכָחַשׁ וְהִתְפּוֹרֵר,
הָלְכָה וְהֶעֱצִימָה הַכְּלִימָה.

וּכְמוֹ שֶׁהָעוֹצֵם עֵינָיו וּמְכַוְּצָן בַּחֹשֶׁךְ בְּמַאֲמָץ גָּדוֹל
רוֹאֶה פִּתְאוֹם כְּתָמִים צִבְעוֹנִיִּים שֶׁל אוֹר,
כָּךְ, בְּחֶשְׁכַת מוֹתוֹ הַמְּאַמֶּצֶת, רָאָה הָאִישׁ הַמֵּת
אֶת רְסִיסֵי הַלַּעַג הַנּוֹקְבִים, אֶת רְצוּדָיו הַמְפַלְחִים,
לַעַג צִבְעוֹנִי, מַפְתִּיעַ, חַז, שְׁלַל צְבָעִים מַרְהִיב -

86

And opposite the night sky chequered with stars beaming –
winking at the magnificence of the universe and its secret,
there is a firmament below, rolling with rollicking skulls –
winking at the horrors of death and its terrors.

And firmament looks at firmament, as in a fun house mirror.
And a man all bent, that goes home alone at night,
seeking a fitting mirror to the burden of his life,
won't raise his head on high and won't wonder at the
    universe's mysteries
only he'll gaze below, for there the sky suits him
and it has no secret, only a piercing pain
and it has no riddle, only a laughable solution,
and there is no dome of blue, only a peel of mockery
where score upon score of horrified grins
shine gleaming from the lower firmament,
like stains of fat from a butcher's filthy apron.

Indeed, it seems shame has no end,
as if death put paid to everything
and only left the insult that wriggles.
And as it grows darker, and there was a dark there
inside of darkness, and as the dead man dies further
and gets lesser, fainter and crumbles
so the shame magnifies.

And as one who shuts his eyes and squints in the darkness
    with great effort
suddenly sees colourful stains of light,
so, in the darkness of his adopted death, the dead man sees
the piercing shards of laughter, its cutting leaps,
colourful mockery, unexpected, sharp, a startling panoply
    of shades –

מַכְאִיב כָּל-כָּךְ, שֶׁאֵין כְּדוּגְמָתוֹ אַף בְּמַחֲזוֹת הָאֵשׁ,
וְכָל עֲטֶרֶת הַצְּבָעִים הַזֹּאת לֹא נִבְרְאָה,
רַק לְקַשֵּׁט אֶת הַכְּאֵב עַל חֶרְפָּתֵנוּ.

וְגַם מִקֵּץ הַרְבֵּה שָׁנִים,
כַּאֲשֶׁר הִתְפּוֹרְרָה גַּם הַגֻּלְגֹּלֶת
וְהָיְתָה לְגַרְגְּרֵי אָבָק, וְרוּחַ
בִּשְׁרִיקָה שֶׁל בּוּז אוֹתָם הֵפִיצָה
לְכָל עֵבֶר, עוֹד נָשָׂא עִמָּם
קוֹל זַעֲקַת הָאִישׁ הַמֵּת, שׁוַעֲה גְּדוֹלָה שֶׁלֹּא תִּתַּם:
הֵי, אַתֶּם לְמַעְלָה, גַּם אֲנִי הָיִיתִי שָׁם!

הַבַּיְתָה חוֹזֵר חֹמֶר עָיֵף,
כָּבִים הָאוֹרוֹת לְאַט,
מִי שֶׁצָּעַק מִתּוֹךְ שְׁנָתוֹ
בְּעֶרֶשׂ עָפָר שָׁקַע, שָׁקַט.

עִם חֲמוֹר וַעֲגָלָה יִשְׂתָּרֵךְ הַמָּשִׁיחַ:
"אַלְטֶע זַאכֶן! אַלְטֶע שׁייעךְ!"

88

so hurtful, that there is nothing like it in the embraces of joy
and all the wreath of these colours was not created
except to decorate the pain of our shame.

And at the end of many years, when even the skull is fallen away
and become flakes of dust, the wind
with a whistle of contempt will cast them out
to every part, and still will be borne with them the sound
of the cry of the dead man,
a moan so great as to never pass:
Hey, you up there, I was here too!

Home goes the tired ass,
the lights go out slow,
whoever cried out in his sleep
in his cradle of earth sank, mute.

With his ass and cart Messiah crawls
and cries out: "Any old iron! Any old shoes!"

כמו בחלוף משב רוח
פואמה קטנה

AS IN A PASSING GUST OF WIND
A small epic

כְּמוֹ בַּחֲלוֹף מַשַּׁב רוּחַ פִּתְאוֹם בְּעַנְפֵי הָעֵץ לְאַחַר שֹׁךְ הַגֶּשֶׁם,
וְרֶגַע יִסְתַּכְסְכוּ הֶעָלִים בִּסְאוֹן שְׁרִיקָה וּרְסִיסֵי מַיִם יִסְפּוּ מֵהֶם
לְמַטָּה בִּנְקִישָׁה אֲטוּמָה עַל פְּנֵי הָאֲדָמָה הָרָוָה, הַטְּמוּמָה,
כָּךְ תּוֹפַע בְּלֵב הָאָדָם מַחֲשֶׁבֶת מָוֶת, בָּאָה פִּתְאוֹם מֵאֵי-אָן,
צֵל מְרַפְרֵף בַּקְּרָבַיִם, מֵטִיל מַחְשָׁךְ פֶּתַע, וּלְרֶגַע יִרְעַד הַלֵּב,
יִנְעֲרוּ-יִסְתַּכְסְכוּ כָּל שַׂרְעַפֵּי הָאָדָם וְדָמָיו לְמַחֲשֶׁבֶת הַכִּלָּיוֹן הַנּוֹרָאָה,
וְשׁוּב שֶׁקֶט הַס, וְשׁוּב יִמָּשְׁכוּ הַחַיִּים בַּמָּקוֹם שֶׁעָצְרוּ, וְהַיָּד
הַתּוֹעָה עַל בְּשַׂר הָאִשָּׁה תָּשׁוּב לִנְסֹעַ אֶל מַחוֹזוֹת עֹנֶג נִכְסָפִים.

וְזֶה דְּבַר מַחֲשֶׁבֶת מָוֶת (מַחֲשָׁבָה נְפוֹצָה, פְּשׁוּטָה, עֲמָמִית אִם תִּרְצוּ):
לַיְלָה אֶחָד, בְּאֶמְצַע נַחֲרַת חָטְמִי הַקְּצוּבָה, נְחִירָה אַחַת תִּקָּטַע.
עֲוִית תֹּאחֵז בַּגּוּף. וְתַחַת הַנְּחִירָה הַמְצַפְצֶפֶת יַעַל חִרְחוּר עָמֹק,
גְּנִיחָה עֲמוּמָה הַבּוֹקַעַת מִתַּחְתִּיּוֹת הַנֶּפֶשׁ הַכָּלָה. אָז אֶפְקַח עֵינַי,
אוֹ שֶׁלֹּא אֶפְקָחֵן. יִהְיֶה פִּרְפּוּר, פְּעִירַת הַפֶּה, טִלְטוּל הָרֹאשׁ
מִצַּד אֶל צַד – וְקָפָא הַכֹּל, וְשֶׁקֶט, דּוּמִיָּה. לֹא יָשׁוּב
הָאַף אֶל צִיּוּצוֹ הַמָּתוֹק, פָּרְחָה לָעַד סְנוּנִית חַיַּי. וַאֲנִי אֶהְיֶה זֶה.
לֹא אִשָּׁה, לֹא חָתוּל, רַק אֲנִי, אֲנִי, לֹא עוֹד שׁוֹשְׁבִין זָחוּחַ לִפְטִירוֹת הַזּוּלַת,

92

As in a passing gust of wind suddenly in branches after the
   slosh of rain
When momentarily the leaves rustle in a whistling hubbub
   and fragments of water fall from them
down in an impenetrable knock on the surface of the
   slaked, hard earth
so shall the thought of death appear in the heart of man, all
   of a sudden from who knows where
a shadow hovering in the gizzard, casting dark all of a
   sudden, and for a moment the heart quakes
all the shivers of a man will rattle and shake, as will his
   blood at the thought of the terrible end
and once more quiet falls and once more life goes on where
   it did pause, and the hand
roaming the woman's flesh will once more resume journeys
   to desirable destinations.

And this is the thing about the thought of death (a common
   thought, simple, popular if you will):
One night, in the middle of my schnozzle's steady snores, a
   single snore will cut to the quick.
A paroxysm will seize the body. And beneath the piping
   snore will rise a deep gurgle,
A dim groan emitting from the depth of the soul expiring.
   Then I'll open my eyes wide,
Or I won't open them. There'll be a flutter, a mouth gaped, a
   head shaken
From side to side – and everything be frozen, and quiet, still.
   No more
Will the nose sound its sweet tweeting, the swallow of my
   life forever flown. And I will be the one.
No woman, no cat, just me, me, no longer a snotty usher at
   another's passing,

כִּי הַפַּעַם חֲתַן הַפְּטִירָה בְּעַצְמוֹ; וַאֲנִי הוּא בַּעַל הַמָּוֶת, בַּעַל הַקֵּץ, בַּעַל סוֹף
הַמִּשְׁמוּשׁ בִּבְשַׂר נָשִׁים, תֹּם הַמִּשְׁמוּשׁ בִּשְׁטָרוֹת הַכֶּסֶף הֶחָמוּד – אֲנִי הוּא.

וְחַיֵּי הַנְּקָלִים יֵאָרוּ לִי לְפֶתַע בְּאוֹר יְקָרוֹת, חַיֵּי הַיָּפִים, הַטּוֹבִים,
חַיַּי, חַיֵּי בָּהֶם הָלַכְתִּי לְזוֹנוֹת; הוֹי זוֹנוֹת וּבַנְקִים,
הוֹי כַּסְפֵּי הַחַי וְהַנּוֹשֵׁם בַּבַּנְק, עוֹלֶה, פּוֹרֵחַ וּמַבְרִיא, וַאֲנִי אֵינֶנִּי.

זוֹ כָּל מַחֲשֶׁבֶת מָוֶת. וּבְשׁוּבֵנוּ אֶל סְאוֹב חַיֵּינוּ הָרָגִיל, וּבְחַטֶּט שׁוּב יָדֵנוּ
בִּבְשַׂר הָאִשָּׁה, "מַה קָּרָה לְךָ?" הִיא שׁוֹאֶלֶת לְלֹא סַקְרָנוּת אֲמִתִּית
עַל דְּבַר הַיָּד שֶׁקָּפְאָה לְפֶתַע, אַךְ אָנוּ בַּכָּתֵף מוֹשְׁכִים, מַה טַּעַם לוֹמַר לָהּ,
הֲלֹא אִישׁ אִישׁ חַי אֶת פְּחָדָיו בְּתוֹרוֹ וּמוֹאֵס בְּפַחֲדֵי הַזּוּלַת;
וּבְכֵן הַיָּד שׁוּב מְגַשֶּׁשֶׁת (הֵי הֲנָאָה מִינִית שְׁפָלָה, אַתְּ, וְגֵרוּד פְּטִירָתִי
בֵּין אֶצְבְּעוֹת הָרֶגֶל, וּמְנָת חֲזֶרֶת חֲרִיפָה, אַתֶּן שָׁלֹשׁ פִּסְגּוֹת עִילָאִיּוֹת שֶׁל עֹנֶג!)
וּכְבָר שׁוֹכַחַת הָאִשָּׁה אֶת שְׁאֵלָתָהּ, וְאָנוּ אֶת הַמָּוֶת שׁוֹכְחִים, וְתֵכֶף וְנִגְּחָה.

פָּתַחְנוּ בִּדְמוּיֵי מִתּוֹךְ הַטֶּבַע, בַּטֶּבַע נְסַיֵּם: נִמְשְׁלוּ מַחְשְׁבוֹתֵינוּ
לְפָרוֹת הַמַּרְעֶה, בְּהֵמוֹת לֹא רְחוֹצוֹת מַעֲלוֹת גֵּרָה. כָּל הַיּוֹם
בָּאֲחוּ הַקָּטָן שֶׁל מֹחֵנוּ שׁוֹטְטוּ עֲצֵלוֹת, עָשׂוּ מֻג, לְחֵכוּ עֵשֶׂב דַּל,
וְהִנֵּה רַד הַיּוֹם, הִתְאָרְכוּ הַצְּלָלִים, שָׁבוֹת הַפָּרוֹת לָרֶפֶת,
בְּפִשְׁפֵּשׁ הַצַּר שֶׁל חֲצַר חֲלוֹמוֹתֵינוּ נִכְנָסוֹת הֵן אַחַת אַחַת, הוֹלְכוֹת
בְּצַעַד אִטִּי, מָדוּז, מַחְשָׁבוֹת פּוֹלִיטִיקָה וּפְלִילִים, זוּטוֹת וּשְׁטֻיּוֹת,

94

But this time the dying groom himself; and I am the master of
   the death, master of the end, master of surcease
Of fondling of women's flesh, the end of groping those cute bank
   notes – I am him.

And my base life will be illuminated for me suddenly in a
   precious light, my beautiful, good life
My life, in which I went to whores; oh to whores and banks,
Oh my money which lives and breathes in a bank, rising,
   blossoming, recovering, but I am no more.

That's all the thought of death. And when we resume the ordure of our
   daily round, and when our hand begins once more to rummage
In the woman's flesh, "What's the matter with you?" she asks
   without real interest
Regarding the hand that froze for a moment, all of a sudden,
   but we shrug our shoulders, what's the point of telling her
for does not each by each live with his own fears in turn and
   revile the fears of his neighbour
and so the hand feels its way once more (hey base sexual pleasure,
   you and scratching athlete's foot between my toes, and a helping
   of strong horseradish are the three plateaus of ecstasy!)
And the woman's already forgetting her question and we forget
   death and any minute we'll be snoring.

We began with a natural simile, back in nature let's conclude:
   our thoughts have been likened
To cows at pasture, unwashed beasts chewing the cud. All day long
In the little meadow of our mind they wandered idly, mooed,
   laved the sparse grass,
And now day is waning, the shadows growing longer, the cows
   return to the dairy
In the narrow wicket of our dream yard they go one by one, plodding
In a steady, measured gait, thoughts of politics and crime,
   bottoms and baggage,

כַּפְתּוֹר וָדֹלַר – מֵרָחוֹק כֻּלָּן כֹּה דוֹמוֹת זוֹ לָזוֹ – אַחֲרֵיהֶן בַּמְאַסֵּף
בְּהֵמָה זְקֵנָה, כֹּה רַבּוֹת כְּבָר הוּבְלוּ לִשְׁחִיטָה וְרַק הִיא נוֹתְרָה,
מוֹשֶׁכֶת בְּעֹל חַיֶּיהָ יוֹם יוֹם, עֶרֶב עֶרֶב, הֲלֹא הִיא
מַחֲשֶׁבֶת צַעַר תְּשׁוּקוֹת בְּשָׂרֵנוּ הַיָּשָׁן וְהַטּוֹבָה.

אָז נוֹתְרָה בַּחוּץ הִיא לְבַד, אַחֲרוֹנָה, פְּרַת צַעַר תְּשׁוּקוֹת בְּשָׂרֵנוּ,
עוֹד עָמְדָה כִּמְעַט קָט, גִּלְגְּלָה עֵינֶיהָ אֶל אֹפֶק הַדְּמְדּוּמִים, שָׁם
דַּם הַשֶּׁמֶשׁ הַלּוֹהֵט פּוֹרֵץ מִבַּעַד תַּחְבּוֹשׁוֹת הָעֲנָנִים הַלְּבָנִים, וּמַה זֶּה
הָיָה שָׁם, מָה רַצֶּה, זַהֲרוּר אוֹר, נִצְנוּץ, רֶשֶׁף אַרְגָּמָן הַבְּלִיחַ, הִכָּה
כְּמוֹ בָּרָק בְּעֵין הַפָּרָה בְּפַחַד אַדִּיר, כִּי הִנֵּה נִרְתְּעָה פִּתְאֹם, וְרֶטֶט
חָלַף בִּבְשָׂרָהּ, אַחַר הִשְׁפִּילָה עֵינֶיהָ נוּגוֹת, הִרְכִּינָה רֹאשָׁהּ, וְחֶרֶשׁ חֶרֶשׁ
הִפְסִיעָה פְּנִימָה, תְּחִלָּה הִיא, אַחֲרֶיהָ זְנָבָהּ, וְנֶעֶלְמָה וְנִסְגַּר הַשַּׁעַר,
וְכָךְ נֶחְתַּם הַיּוֹם; כֵּן, הָיְתָה כָּאן מַחֲשֶׁבֶת מָוֶת, אֲבָל הִיא חָלְפָה,
וְאֶת יוֹמֵנוּ – כְּמוֹ גַם אֶת שִׁירֵנוּ – מְסַיֵּם אֵיזֶה צַעַר סָתוּם, בַּהֲמִי וְכָבֵד,
הַלּוֹבֵשׁ לְעֵינֵינוּ תָּמִיד אֶת דְּמֻיוֹת הַנָּשִׁים הַהוֹלְכוֹת מֵאִתָּנוּ;
אֲהָהּ, הַבָּשָׂר הֶעָבֶה הַנִּפְלָא, הַמָּלֵא גַּרְגּוּרֵי צְחוֹק גַּס וְעֹנֶג, וְאָרוּז בִּשְׂמָלוֹת,
תָּמִיד הַשְּׂמָלוֹת הַנִּפְרָשׂוֹת שׁוּב וָשׁוּב כְּמוֹ מְנִיפָה נִצְחִית
מֵעַל רֹאשֵׁנוּ הַנּוֹפֵל אֲחוֹרָה בְּלִי חַיִּים.

96

A button and a dime – from afar they look all alike –
   behind them in the coral
An old beast of burden, so many now led to slaughter and
   only she is left behind,
Dragging the yoke of her life day by day, nightfall by
   nightfall, for it's she
The thought of the sorrow of our flesh's lust, so old and good.

Then only she remains beyond, alone, the last, sorrowful
   cow of our flesh's yearning,
She still stood there a little while, rolled her eyes to the
   distant dimming, out there
The sun's hot blood bursts past the clouds' white bandages,
   and what's that
Over there, what glazed, a spark of light, a glimmer of
   purple flickered, struck
Like lightning in the cow's eye a terrible fear, for look she's
   suddenly withdrawn, and a quiver
Passed through her flesh, then she dropped her sad eyes,
   lowered her neck and softly softly
Padded in, first her, then her tail, and she's disappeared
   and the gate's closing
And so the day is sealed; yes, there was a thought of death
   here, but it passed,
And our day – just like our poem – will be concluded with
   some blocked, bestial, leaden hurt,
Which puts on for our eyes always the image of the women
   walking away;
Ah the splendid thick flesh, full of gurgles of coarse
   laughter and pleasure, and packed in frocks
Always the frocks spreading again and again like the
   eternal lace fan
Over our head falling back without life.

חרוזי פרידה לאהובה

PARTING LIMERICKS TO A LOVER

זוֹ שָׁעָה נִפְלָאָה

שֶׁל רַעֲדַת הַלֵּב,
וְהָיִיתִי רוֹעֵד לוּ יָכֹלְתִּי לִרְעֹד,
וְהָיִיתִי שָׁר וְלוֹחֵשׁ בְּאָזְנַיִךְ
לוּ יָכֹלְתִּי לָשִׁיר וְלִלְחֹשׁ,
זוֹ שָׁעָה נִפְלָאָה,
לֹא הָיְתָה, לֹא תִהְיֶה עוֹד כְּמוֹתָהּ,
אַתְּ גּוֹהֶרֶת עָלַי, וַאֲנִי תַּחְתַּיִךְ
קָשׁוּב בְּלִי תְּנוּעָה,
כְּאִלּוּ יִהְיֶה עוֹד רֶגַע דְּבַר-מָה,
שֶׁכְּמוֹתוֹ לֹא יָדַעְתִּי,
וְאַתְּ עוֹד תֵּדְעִי,
וַאֲנִי לֹא אֵדַע.

אני מחרחר במיטה

אֲנִי מְחַרְחֵר בַּמִּטָּה,
מַצָּבִי לֹא טוֹב,
אֲהוּבָתִי מְשׂוֹחַחַת עַל כָּךְ בַּפְּרוֹזְדּוֹר
עִם הַיָּדִיד צְבִי וְהַמַּכָּר דֹּב.

IT'S A WONDERFUL HOUR

Of heart's tremors
And I would have trembled if I could still tremble,
And I would have sung and whispered in your ear,
If only I could sing and whisper,
That wonderful hour
Was not, there never will be another like it,
You bent over me and me beneath
Listening without a stir,
As if there would any minute be something,
Of the sort I had never known,
And you will still know it,
But I will not know anything.

I'M GURGLING IN BED

I'm gurgling in bed
My condition isn't good,
My love is discussing it in the hall
With her friend Zvi and acquaintance Dov.

חשבתי שאצלנו זה יהיה שונה

חָשַׁבְתִּי שֶׁאֶצְלֵנוּ זֶה יִהְיֶה שׁוֹנֶה:
כְּשֶׁהָרוֹפְאִים יֹאמְרוּ: "הוּא מֵת" -
אַתְּ לֹא תַרְפִּי,
שָׁעוֹת, יָמִים, שָׁנִים
עוֹד תִּגְהֲרִי עָלַי,
פִּיךְ צָמוּד אֶל פִּי.

אַךְ כְּשֶׁאָמְרוּ לָךְ הָרוֹפְאִים: "הוּא מֵת" -
פָּרַצְתְּ בִּבְכִי וְאַחַר-כָּךְ דָּמַמְתְּ,
שֶׁפֵּרוּשׁוֹ לֹא קַמְתְּ, לֹא הִתְקוֹמַמְתְּ,
שֶׁפֵּרוּשׁוֹ הִשְׁלַמְתְּ, שֶׁפֵּרוּשׁוֹ
אֲנִי לְשָׁם, וְאַתְּ לְשָׁם.

כשליקקתי לך בין הרגליים

כְּשֶׁלִּקַּקְתִּי לָךְ בֵּין הָרַגְלַיִם
חָשַׁבְנוּ שֶׁהַזְּמָן עוֹמֵד;
יָבֵשׁ לִקּוּק, הָלְכָה הַמְּלַקֶּקֶת,
הַמְלַקֵּק מֵת.

I THOUGHT WITH US IT WOULD BE DIFFERENT

I thought with us it would be different:
That when they doctors said: "He's dead" –
You would not let go,
For hours, days, years
Stay bent over me
Mouth pressed to my mouth.

But when the doctors said: "He's dead" –
You burst into tears and then grew still,
Which is to say you never rose, didn't rebel,
Which is to say you came to terms, which is to say
I'm over here, you're over there.

WHEN I LICKED YOU BETWEEN THE LEGS

When I licked you between the legs
We thought that time stood still;
The lick ran dry, the lickee went away
The licker ceased to be.

אהיה בתוך המון עצום

אֶהְיֶה בְּתוֹךְ הָמוֹן עָצוּם
תּוֹפֵס לִי נֶפַח בְּצִמְצוּם,
לְאַט נִפְתָּח, לְאַט נִכְנָס,
כָּל הָעִנְיָן פָּשׁוּט וְנַס,
כְּמוֹ אֶנְקַת אַהֲבָתֵךְ
כְּשֶׁפִּי בְּפִי-טַבַּעְתֵּךְ,
כְּמוֹ חִרְחוּר אַהֲבָתִי
הַמְהַדְהֵד כִּצְלִיל מוֹתִי.

כשראתה אהובתי

כְּשֶׁרָאֲתָה אֲהוּבָתִי אֵיךְ טוֹמְנִים אוֹתִי בְּבוֹר לֹא-עָמֹק,
בְּדִיּוּק נִכְנַס לָהּ בָּרֹחַשׁ לַתַּחַת שֶׁלָּהּ הַמָּתוֹק,
וְאָז נַעֲשׂוּ שְׁנֵי מַעֲשִׂים בְּיָקוּם בַּד בְּבַד,
נִבְכְּתָה לוֹ בְּכִי גָּדוֹל וְגֵרוּד קָטָן גֵּרַד.

104

I'LL BE AMONG A VAST MULTITUDE

I'll be among a vast multitude
Taking up minimal space
Slowly reducing, slowly being bitten
The whole thing simple and plain
Like your love cry
When my mouth is in your ring,
Like my love groan
Echoing as my dying sound.

WHEN MY LOVE SAW

When my love saw them
Put me in the shallow hole
Just then something crept
In her sweet behind
And then two deeds were
In the universe done at once
A great weeping was wept
And a small itch was scratched.

אני מתחת, את מעל

אֲנִי מִתַּחַת, אַתְּ מֵעַל,
אַתְּ הִפְעִיל, אֲנִי נִפְעָל,
אַתְּ בָּשָׂר, אֲנִי תְּמוּנָה,
אֲנִי אֵינֶנּוּ, אַתְּ יֶשְׁנָהּ.

אני חוזר אל אבי ואמי

אֲנִי חוֹזֵר אֶל אָבִי וְאִמִּי,
הֵם חִכּוּ לִי וּבָאתִי.
אִתָּךְ הָיָה נִסָּיוֹן רָפֶה
לַעֲבֹר אֶת גִּיל תֵּשַׁע -
הוּא לֹא עָלָה יָפֶה.
אֲנִי חוֹזֵר אֶל אָבִי וְאִמִּי.

106

I'M BELOW, YOU'RE ABOVE

I'm below, you're above,
You're active, I'm acted on,
You're flesh, I'm image,
I'm gone, you're still there.

I'M GOING BACK TO MY MUM AND DAD

I'm going back to my Mum and Dad.
They waited for me and I returned.
With you there was a faint attempt
To get past the age of nine –
It didn't turn out right
I'm going back to my Mum and Dad.

אני בשכיבה

אֲנִי בִּשְׁכִיבָה,
מֵעָלַי שָׁכְבָה,
מֵעָלֶיהָ יָשְׁבוּ,
מֵעָלָיו מַחֲשָׁבָה:
"שָׁלוֹם, אַהֲבָה".

תמתי לגווע

תַּמְתִּי לִגְוֹעַ.
בַּלַּיְלָה אָבוֹא אֵלַיִךְ,
אִישׁ לֹא גָּבוֹהַּ,
לְקַנֵּן בַּחֲלוֹמֵךְ.

אֲהוּבָתִי, חֶמְדַּת חַיַּי,
אֲשֶׁר נַפְשִׁי יָצְאָה אֵלַיִךְ,
אֲשֶׁר בִּנְשִׁיקָתֵךְ לִבִּי פָּג -
חִלְמִי עָלַי.

108

I'M LYING DOWN

I'm lying down,
Above me a stratum,
Above that a bottom,
Above that a refrain:
"Goodbye, darling."

I HAVE CEASED TO EXPIRE

I have ceased to expire.
At night I'll come to you,
A man not so tall,
To build nests in your dream.

My love, my life's delight,
To whom my soul went out
In whose kiss my heart melted –
Dream of me a while.

אהובה, בפי הטבעת

אֲהוּבָה, בְּפִי הַטַּבַּעַת
הִשְׁאַרְתִּי לָךְ לקוּק,
שָׁמְרִי עָלָיו עוֹד רֶגַע,
קְצָת אָפוּק,
יוֹם שֶׁל עֲצִירוּת,
כַּוּוּץ, עִנּוּי, עִנּוּג,
וְאָז - אָפוּג.

בלילות אני בוכה מגעגועים

בַּלֵּילוֹת אֲנִי בּוֹכֶה מִגַּעְגוּעִים,
אִם כִּי אֵין לִי עֵינַיִם לִבְכּוֹת –
חוֹשֵׁב - אֲבָל אֵין לִי גַּם מֹחַ לַחֲשֹׁב –
עַל אוֹרוֹת הָעִיר, עַל הַזְּמָן שֶׁצָּחַקְנוּ.

לוּ רַק יָדַעְתְּ, לוּ רַק יָדַעְתְּ,
אִשָׁה שֶׁלִּי, אֲהוּבַת נַפְשִׁי,
אֵיךְ אֲבַלֶּה אֶת מוֹתִי בַּקֶּבֶר,
אֵיךְ אַגִּיד לָךְ, אֵיךְ אֶכְתֹּב שִׁיר?

MY LOVE, IN THE RING'S MOUTH

My love, in the ring's mouth
I've left you a lick
Keep it another moment,
A little restraint,
A day of gut ache,
Constriction, ecstasy, torture,
And then – I'll disappear.

AT NIGHT I WEEP WITH LONGING

At night I weep with longing
For all that I've no eyes to weep with –
Think – but have no brain to think –
About the city lights, about the time we laughed.

If only you knew, if only you knew
My wife, my soul's passion,
How I will spend my death in the grave,
How shall I tell you, how shall I write this song?

את מי אהבה אהובתי

אֶת מִי אָהֲבָה אֲהוּבָתִי? –
אֲהוּבָתִי אָהֲבָה אוֹתִי;
אֶת מִי אוֹהֶבֶת אֲהוּבָתִי? –
אֶת זֶה שֶׁלּוֹחֵשׁ בְּאָזְנָהּ עַכְשָׁו:
הוֹי אֲהוּבָתִי, אֲהוּבָתִי.

אהובתי, כאן חושך

אֲהוּבָתִי, כָּאן חֹשֶׁךְ,
הָאֲדָמָה עַל עֵינֵי מְהֻדֶּקֶת,
אֲנִי לֹא רוֹאֶה עִם מִי אַתְּ מִתְחַבֶּקֶת,
לְמִי אַתְּ לוֹחֶשֶׁת מִלִּים נִפְלָאוֹת,
שֶׁהָיוּ רַק שֶׁלִּי, וְעַכְשָׁו גַּם שֶׁלּוֹ.

112

WHO DID MY LOVE LOVE

Who did my love love?
My love loved me;
Who does my love love?
The one who's now whispering in her ear:
Oh my love, my love.

MY LOVE, IT'S DARK HERE

My love, it's dark here
The ground on my eyes is fastened
I do not see who you've embraced,
Who you're whispering to those sweet words
That were only mine, and now are also his.

בלכתך מעימי, אהובה

בְּלֶכְתֵּךְ מֵעִמִּי, אֲהוּבָה,
מִתְחַכְּכִים אֶצְלֵךְ שְׁנֵי חֶלְקֵי הָעַכּוּז,
מַתִּיזִים אֶל קִבְרִי גֵּץ קָטָן שֶׁל בּוּז.

כשחיבקת חזק את צוארי

כְּשֶׁחִבַּקְתְּ חָזָק אֶת צַוָּארִי
בְּיָדַיִךְ הַצְּבוּעוֹת לַכָּה,
מֵעַיִךְ הַגְּדוֹשִׁים קָקָה
זִמְּרוּ: יִהְיוּ אֲחֵרִים.

WHEN YOU GO FROM ME, MY LOVE

When you go from me, my love
Your two sections of buttock scuffle
And spark towards my grave a tiny spark of derision.

WHEN YOU CLASPED MY NECK TIGHT

When you clasped my neck tight
With your hands painted with polish,
Your bowels that were crammed with piss,
Sang out: there will be others.

אהובה שלי, אמרי, היכן את

אֲהוּבָה שֶׁלִּי, אִמְרִי, הֵיכָן אַתְּ,
מוּל מִי נִפְשָׁק כָּעֵת פִּי הַטַּבַּעַת,
וְלֹא שֶׁלֹּא אָהַבְתִּי בָּךְ אֶת הַנְּשָׁמָה,
אֲבָל הַחוֹר הַהוּא מֵצִיק לִי מִשּׁוּם-מָה.

את משתינה על פני האדמה

אַתְּ מַשְׁתִּינָה עַל פְּנֵי הָאֲדָמָה,
אֲנִי שׁוֹכֵב בְּפֶה פָּעוּר תַּחְתֶּיהָ,
זֶה לֹא מַה שֶּׁדִּבַּרְנוּ וְתִכְנַנּוּ,
זֶה לֹא מַה שֶּׁהִבְטַחְתָּ, חַבֵּק, נָשַׁק,
כִּי עַל אוֹתוֹ מִישׁוֹר הָיִינוּ שְׁנֵינוּ,
עַל אוֹתָהּ מִטָּה צָהַלְנוּ, הִתְגּוֹלַלְנוּ,
אַךְ בַּגְּסִיסָה נָתַתִּי בָּךְ מַבָּט רָפֶה:
"אַתְּ תַּשְׁתִּינִי, אֲנִי אֶפְעַר פֶּה".

MY LOVE, TELL ME, WHERE ARE YOU

My love, tell me, where are you
Before whom is the orifice now opening?
And not that I didn't love your soul
But that hole is bothering me for some reason.

YOU'RE PISSING ON THE FACE OF THE GROUND

You piss on the face of the ground,
I'm lying open-mouthed beneath it,
That's not what we discussed and planned
It's not what was promised, hugged, kissed,
For on the same plane we were two,
On the same bed we cheered and grappled,
But with my expiration I gave you a wan glance:
"You will piss and I will open my mouth."

מעל איש נרקב

מֵעַל אִישׁ נִרְקָב
בְּבוֹר נָאֱלָח
אֲהוּבָה יְפַת-קַו
עִם חוֹר לַח.

אני נפרד ליסודותי

אֲנִי נִפְרָד לִיסוֹדוֹתַי,
מִתְפָּרֵק יְסוֹד-יְסוֹד,
מַשְׁמִיעַ צְקְסְקְס אָרֹךְ שֶׁל נוֹד,
אַתְּ נִפְרֶדֶת מֵעָלַי,
זָז הַתַּחַת - הוֹף וְהוֹפָה,
עוֹד אֶתְמוֹל בּוֹכָה בְּאַסְיָה -
הַיּוֹם גּוֹנַחַת בְּאֵירוֹפָּה.

ABOVE A ROTTING MAN

Above a rotting man
In a filthy hole
A sweet-assed beloved
With a moist aperture.

I'M DECOMPOSING TO MY CONSTITUENT PARTS

I'm decomposing to my constituent parts
Decomposing to constituent by constituent
Sounding a long hiss of regret,
You are taking your leave
The ass is on the move – hippity hopa.
Only yesterday in Asia she wept
Today she's groaning in Europa.

בקו אחד עם הביוב

בְּקַו אֶחָד עִם הַבִּיוּב
אֲנִי שׁוֹכֵב, חָטְמִי זָקוּף,
וּכְשֶׁעוֹבֶרֶת צוֹאָתֵךְ,
חוֹלֵף בִּי רַעַד, כְּמוֹ לְטוּף.

עשור למותי בערך

עָשׂוֹר לְמוֹתִי בְּעֶרֶךְ,
תָּבוֹאִי לְבַקֵּר עִם פֶּרַח,
וּלְצִדֵּךְ צֵל צָנוּעַ.
וַאֲנִי אֶשְׁאַל:
– מִי הָאִידְיוֹט?
וְאַתְּ תַּעֲנִי:
– יְהוֹשֻׁעַ רוֹט;
בַּעֲלִי הַיָּקָר יְהוֹשֻׁעַ,
שֶׁעָשָׂה לִי גַּם קְצָת שַׁעֲשׁוּעַ,
מִמֶּנּוּ יָצְאוּ יְלָדֵינוּ
חֵן, תֹּם וּפוּעָה.

120

ON A LEVEL WITH THE DRAINS

On a level with the drains
I'm lying, my schnozzle upraised,
When your movement goes past my face
A tremor runs through me, like a caress.

A DECADE AFTER MY DEATH GIVE OR TAKE

A decade after my death give or take
You'll come to visit with a flower
And beside you a humble shade.
"Who's the idiot?" I'll inquire.
And you'll reply: Joshua Roth
My dear husband Joshua
Who also gave me a little joy
From him came our children
Grace, Tom and Maya.

כשתחשכנה עיני

כְּשֶׁתֶּחְשַׁכְנָה עֵינַי,
שַׁאֲבִי אֶת עֵינַי הַמֵּתוֹת
אֶל עֵינַיִךְ הַפְּקוּחוֹת,
וְקַבְּלִי אֶת מַרְאַי הַמּוּטָל לְחֵיקֵךְ,
וַעֲשִׂי לִי מָקוֹם כִּי קַר,
כִּי אָהַבְתִּי לִהְיוֹת בְּחֻמֵּךְ,
וְעַכְשָׁו כְּבָר רָחוֹק מִמֵּךְ,
וְעַכְשָׁו זֶה נִגְמַר,
וְלֹא יִהְיֶה עוֹד,
וְלֹא נִתְחַבֵּק עוֹד, כִּי תַם,
כִּי נִגְמַר, שַׁאֲבִי אֶת עֵינַי
הַמֵּתוֹת אֶל עֵינַיִךְ,
שָׁם אֶהְיֶה עוֹד מְעַט,
אֵרָאֶה בְּעֵינַיִךְ הַחַיּוֹת, הָרוֹאוֹת,
יֵרָאֶה הָעוֹלָם שֶׁאֵינֶנִּי רוֹאֶה,
שֶׁהָיָה כֹּה אָהוּב, וְעַכְשָׁו
הוּא אָבַד לִי, וְלֹא יִהְיֶה,
רַק עֵינַי הַמֵּתוֹת בְּעֵינַיִךְ הָרוֹאוֹת,
בְּעֵינַיִךְ הַחַיּוֹת עֵינַי הַמֵּתוֹת
חַיּוֹת עוֹד מְעַט, כָּל עוֹד
תִּחְיִי גַּם אַתְּ, כָּל עוֹד
תִּזְכְּרִי, כָּל עוֹד.

WHEN MY EYES GROW DIM

When my eyes grow dim
Draw my dead eyes
Into your open eyes
And take my sight that's thrown in your bosom
And make me some room for it's cold,
For I loved to be in your warmth
And now I'm so far away from you
And now it's over,
And there'll be no more,
We'll not hug more, because it's over
It's done, draw my eyes up
That are dead, into your eyes
There I'll rest for a little while,
See with your living, seeing eyes
There will be a world to see that I don't see
That used to be so beloved, and now
Is lost to me, and will not be
Only my dead eyes in your eyes see
In your living eyes my dead eyes living
for a little longer, so long
As you remember, so long.

PARTING LETTERS TO A LOVER

מכתבי פרידה לאהובה

חדר המכונות של האהבה

הַתְּנוּחָה הַמְפֻרְסֶמֶת שֶׁל הָאַהֲבָה: הָרֹאשׁ מֻרְכָּן, גַּחוּן נִזְעָם-מִתְרַפֵּס עַל הַפָּנִים, וְהַגּוּף כִּמְעַט מְקֻפָּל לִשְׁנַיִם מֵחֲמַת הַמַּכָּה הָאַדִירָה שֶׁסָּפַגְתָּ בְּבִטְנְךָ.

וְכָךְ, שָׁפוּף, צִיצִית שַׂעֲרוֹתֶיךָ כִּמְעַט שְׁנּוֹגַעַת בָּרִצְפָּה, אַתָּה יוֹרֵד בַּסֻּלָּם לְמַטָּה, אֶל חֲדַר הַמְכוֹנוֹת שֶׁל הָאַהֲבָה: כָּאן מַרְגִּישִׁים רַע, הָאֲוִיר סָמִיךְ, מָלֵא אֵדִים קָשִׁים. כָּאן עוֹבְדִים בְּמִשְׁמָרוֹת רְצוּפוֹת, יָמִים וְלֵילוֹת, בְּפִיחַ, בְּמַחֲנָק וּבְזֵעָה. לֹא תֵאָרְנוּ לְעַצְמֵנוּ שֶׁכָּל-כָּךְ קָשֶׁה יִהְיֶה. בַּמַּגְזִינִים הֶרְאוּ לָנוּ אִיִּים שְׁלֵוִים, זְרִיחוֹת וּשְׁקִיעוֹת מַרְהִיבוֹת. מַה לִּי וְלָהֶם? אֲנִי שָׁקוּעַ עַד צַוָּאר בַּעֲמָלִי הַמְפָרֵךְ. הַשָּׁאוֹן מַחֲרִישׁ אָזְנַיִם, הֲלֹא גַּם אִם אֶצְוַח כָּאן בְּכָל כֹּחִי: "אֲנִי אוֹהֵב אוֹתָךְ!" – מִי יִשְׁמַע? עֵינַי צוֹרְבוֹת, יֵשׁ לַעֲמֹל בִּשְׂפָתַיִם חֲשׂוּקוֹת, לְהַגִּיר זֵעָה. מִזְּמַן אֵינִי שׁוֹאֵל: הֵיכָן אֲנִי? לְאָן אַגִּיעַ?

THE ENGINE ROOM OF LOVE

The famous attitude of love: head reclined, a furious-pleading chortle on your face, and your body almost doubled over from the force of the tremendous blow to your stomach.

And so, crouched, the tuft of your hair almost touching the floor, you go down the ladder, to the engine room of love: here it feels bad, the air is viscous, full of difficult echoes. Here they work continuous shifts, day and night, in the soot, in the choke and sweat. We never imagined it would be so hard. In magazines they showed us tranquil isles, dazzling sunrises and sunsets. What have I to do with these? I'm up to my neck in back-breaking graft. The din is deafening my ears, even if I screamed for all I'm worth "I love you!" Who would hear? Eyes burning, you've to work with pursed lips to work up a sweat. For a long time now I haven't asked: Where am I? Where will I come to be?

שאיבת דמותך אל מוח הנועד לכיליון

בְּשִׁבְתֵּנוּ יַחַד לַשֻּׁלְחָן, אוֹ בְּהָלְכֵנוּ בָּרְחוֹב, אֲנִי מוֹצֵץ אוֹתָךְ אֶל קִרְבִּי, יַתּוּשׁ עֲנָק הַתּוֹקֵעַ בָּךְ אֶת מְשׁוֹשָׁיו, יוֹנֵק וְיוֹנֵק אֶת דָּמֵךְ. אָטוּם לָעוֹלָם כֻּלּוֹ, אֵין לִי אֶלָּא מַרְאֵךְ שֶׁלָּךְ. רַק אוֹתָךְ, אוֹתָךְ אֲנִי זוֹלֵל, בָּךְ אֲנִי מִתְפַּטֵּם, בְּבוֹלְעָנוּת שֶׁאֵין לָהּ גְּבוּל, לֹא שָׂבֵעַ לְעוֹלָם.

וּמְשֶׁהִתְמַלֵּאתִי, אֲנִי פּוֹרֵשׁ לִי לַפִּנָּה וּמְעַכֵּל אֶת תְּנוּעוֹתַיִךְ וּמִלּוֹתַיִךְ, אֶת כָּל רְסִיסֵי דְמוּתֵךְ, לִפְרָטֵי פְּרָטִים. הַכֹּל רָשׁוּם, הַכֹּל נִבְנֶה וּמְפֹרָק, נִטְחָן וּמֻדְבָּק שׁוּב וָשׁוּב בְּעָמָל אֵין קֵץ.

בְּמֹחִי הַכֹּל, בְּמֹחִי, אַךְ לֹא לִזְמָן רַב. דְּמוּתֵךְ נִשְׁאֶבֶת אֶל מֹחַ הַנּוֹעַד לְכִלָּיוֹן. גֹּדֶשׁ פְּרָטַיִךְ, תִּפְאַרְתֵּךְ, כָּל הַמִּלּאי הָאַדִּיר הַמְאֻחְסָן בְּעַרְבּוּבְיָה, הַתִּפְאוּרָה הָעֲנָקִית שֶׁנִּבְנְתָה בְּעָמָל אַדִּירִים, הַכֹּל יִתְפּוֹרֵר לְאָבָק דַּק. מַה עַל מַאֲמַצֵּי הַבְּנִיָּה וְהַשִּׁמּוּר? הֵיכָן מִפְעַל הָאַהֲבָה? הֲלֹא הָגִיתִי בָּךְ וְעִצַּבְתִּי אוֹתָךְ בְּדִמְיוֹנִי לְפָחוֹת כְּמוֹ מִסְפַּר הַבִּנְיָנִים בִּכְרַךְ עֲנָק – תְּאָרֵי לָךְ מִין פָּארִיז שֶׁכָּל חֲזִיתוֹת בָּתֶּיהָ מְכֻסּוֹת דֹּק רַךְ שֶׁל אֲרֶשֶׁת פָּנַיִךְ! - פָּארִיז זוֹ תֶּחֱרַב.

אַתְּ רוֹאָה רַק אֶת פִּי הַיּוֹנֵק הַמְלַכְלֵךְ בְּדָמֵךְ; אֵינֵךְ שׁוֹמַעַת אֶת הָאֲנָחָה הַמְלַוָּה אֶת הַיְּנִיקָה, כִּמְעַט בִּלְתִּי נִשְׁמַעַת, מוּזִיקַת הַמֹּחַ הַיּוֹדֵעַ עַל עֲמַל הַשָּׁוְא שֶׁל הַפֶּה.

וּבְעוֹד אַתְּ יְשֵׁנָה - עַכְשָׁו מֻקְדָּם בַּבֹּקֶר - וּמֹחֵךְ מַגִּיר עֲסִיס חֲלוֹמוֹת, מֹחִי שֶׁלִּי זָב אֶת צַעַר הָאָבְדָן. שִׁמְעִי אֶת הַמֹּחַ הַמְקוֹנֵן חֶרֶשׁ אֶת קִינָתוֹ.

DRAWING YOUR IMAGE INTO A MIND SCHEDULED FOR ANNIHILATION

When we sit at a table together, or walk in the street, I suck you inside of me, a huge mosquito sticking you with its feelers, suckling and suckling on your blood. Impervious to the whole world, I have nothing but the sight of you. Just you, you I guzzle, on you I feast, with a greed that knows no bounds, never satisfied.

And when I'm filled, I retire to a corner to digest your stirs and words, all the smithereens of your image, in minute detail, everything is taken down, everything is built and dismantled, ground down and stuck together again and again in never-ending toil.

In my mind everything exists, in my mind but not for long. Your image is drawn into a mind bound for extinction. Overflowing with your details, your magnificence, all the tremendous stock inventoried in the topsy-turvy, giant scenery built with enormous toil, will all crumble to dust so miniscule. What about the efforts in construction, the upkeep? Where is the factory of love? Have I not conceived you and styled you in my fancy at least like a few buildings in a giant metropolis – imagine a kind of Paris where the storefronts of all the houses are covered with a soft scrim of the expression on your face! This Paris will fall to ruins.

You see only the mouth of the filthy suckler in your blood, you do not hear the sigh that accompanies the suckling, almost beyond hearing, the music of the mind that knows about the fruitless labour of the mouth.

And while you're still asleep – now early in the morning – and your mind shedding juicy dreams, my mind is suppurating the sorrow of loss. Listen to my mind quietly keening its keens.

הלוחם

כְּמֵעֵין תְּרוּעָה נִשְׁמַעַת בְּתוֹכִי, מְזַעֲזַעַת אֶת יְשׁוּתִי, וּמַשֶּׁהוּ מִזְדַּקֵּף בִּי קוֹמְמִיּוּת, מוּכָן לְהִלָּחֵם. כְּאָדָם קַדְמוֹנִי אֲנִי, אוֹ כְּאִינְדְיָאנִי מָשׁוּחַ בְּצִבְעֵי קְרָב גַּסִּים, מְנֻפְּנָף בְּקַרְדֹּם. נֶגֶד מִי? אֵיפֹה הָאוֹיֵב?

בְּתוֹכִי, כְּמוֹ בֻּבָּה בְּתוֹךְ בֻּבָּה, אֶלֶף אִינְדְיָאנִים, כָּל אֶחָד חִוֵּר יוֹתֵר, מָשׁוּחַ בְּפָחוֹת צְבָעִים מִזֶּה הַחִיצוֹנִי לוֹ, עֲמִידָתוֹ מְהֻסֶּסֶת יוֹתֵר, עַד שֶׁמַּגִּיעִים לְאִינְדְיָאנִי לָבָן מֵאֹד, שֶׁמָּא צְהַבְהַב, יָשִׁישׁ אוֹ יְשִׁישָׁה מוֹנְגּוֹלִית, וּבְתוֹכָהּ יְשִׁישׁוֹת נוֹסָפוֹת, כְּבָר מִזְמָן לֹא מוֹנְגּוֹלִיּוֹת, אַדְרַבָּא, נַעֲשׂוֹת יוֹתֵר וְיוֹתֵר בְּנוֹת עַמֵּנוּ, וּמַגִּיעִים לַבַּסּוֹף, בַּחֵלֶק הַפְּנִימִי, לְזִקְנָה גְּבֶנֶת, וּבְתוֹכָהּ אֶלֶף זְקֵנוֹת הַנַּעֲשׂוֹת יוֹתֵר וְיוֹתֵר יַלְדּוּתִיּוֹת, בָּבוֹת לִפְנִים מִבָּבוֹת שֶׁל יְלָדִים, אֶחָד מְבַעֵת מִמִּשְׁנֵהוּ, עַד שֶׁתַּגִּיעַ לַמֶּרְכָּז, שָׁם הַיֶּלֶד הַמֻּבְהָל וְהַנִּכְשָׁל. אַלְפֵי בָּבוֹת נֶאֱלַצְנוּ לְקַלֵּף עַד שֶׁהִגַּעְנוּ לַגַּרְעִין, וְאַף זֶה עֲדַיִן לֹא הַגַּרְעִין מַמָּשׁ, הֲלֹא בְּתוֹךְ הַיֶּלֶד הַנִּשְׁנָק כְּבָר אֵין דְּמוּת כְּלָל, שָׁם מְפַרְפֶּרֶת הַמַּהוּת שֶׁל הָאֵימָה, יְדִיעַת הַכִּשָּׁלוֹן, הַהִנְהוּן הַבִּלְתִּי-פוֹסֵק לַנּוֹרָא מִכֹּל.

כְּשֶׁנָּגַעְתִּי בָּךְ, מַצְמִיד אֵלַיִךְ בְּחָזְקָה אֶת מִצְחִי, הִצְלַחְתִּי לַעֲצֹר אֶת הַסֶּרֶט.

THE FIGHTER

A kind of trumpet call is heard inside me, shaking my consciousness and something straightens up in me, ready to fight. I'm like a primordial man, or an Indian daubed with gaudy war paints, waving a cudgel. At who? Where's the enemy?

Inside me, like a doll inside a doll, a thousand Indians, each paler than the other, daubed with fewer paints than the one outside him, his posture more hesitant, till you get to the very pale Indian, perhaps jaundiced, a Mongol Mum or Dad, and inside it several more old timers, already a long time not Mongols, *au contraire*, turning more and more to girls of our own kind, and reaching finally to the internal part, to an old hunchback woman, and inside her a thousand old women becoming more and more childish, dolls inside of children's dolls, each exposing its neighbour, until you reach the centre, there the child is frightened and failing. Thousands of dolls we had to peel till we reached the core, and even this is still not the real center, for within the child that's left there's already no image at all, there wriggling is the meaning of terror, the knowledge of failure, the never-ending nod at the most terrible of all.

When I touched you, pressing my fore-head hard to you, I managed to stop the tremor.

נידון לכליאה בצינוק נצחי

נִדּוֹן בַּחֲמָרָה לִכְלִיאָה בְּצִינוֹק לָנֶצַח, וְכָל זֶה רַק מִפְּנֵי שֶׁמַּתִּי. וַהֲרֵי לֹא עָשִׂיתִי רַע לְאִישׁ, אַדְרַבָּא, נֶחְלַשְׁתִּי יוֹתֵר וְיוֹתֵר עַד שֶׁהִתְאַבַּנְתִּי לַיְלָה אֶחָד לְחֵפֶץ דּוֹמֵם. עַל כָּךְ אַתֶּם מוֹבִילִים אוֹתִי בְּפָמַלְּבֵּי, עֲדַת סוֹחֲרִים וְעֵדִים וְצוֹפִים, וְאַתֶּם בֵּינֵיהֶם, לְהַכְלָא בְּצִינוֹק הָאֲדָמָה. אַתֶּם תֵּצְאוּ מִשָּׁם, אֲנִי לֹא. בְּלִי קוֹל אֲנִי לוֹחֵשׁ לָךְ, בְּעוֹדִי מְקֻפְצָץ לִי עַל הָעֲגָלָה הַשְּׁחֹרָה בַּדֶּרֶךְ לַבּוֹר:

"יוֹדַעַת אַתְּ, אֵין טַעַם שֶׁנַּעֲמִיד פָּנִים, אַתְּ עוֹזֶבֶת אוֹתִי. אֲנִי נִדּוֹן לְמַעֲמָד רַע מִזֶּה שֶׁל הַמַּקְקִּים הָרוֹחֲשִׂים עַל צִינוֹרוֹת הַשּׁוֹפְכִין שֶׁלָּךְ. חֲלוֹם כָּמוֹס מְמַלֵּא אֶת לִבִּי – לַעֲמֹד שָׁם בִּמְקוֹמָם, רָתוּק אֶל הַצִּינוֹרוֹת, אֵינִי רַשַּׁאי לָזוּז, כָּל חַיַּי צְפִיָּה לְמַיִם, מֵימַיִךְ, הַנּוֹפְלִים בַּצִּינוֹרוֹת לְאַחַר שֶׁהִתְרַחַצְתְּ אוֹ עָשִׂית אֶת צְרָכַיִךְ, לָדַעַת שֶׁלֹּא תַם עִנְיָנֵנוּ הַמְשֻׁתָּף עֲלֵי אֲדָמוֹת. מְחַיֵּךְ קַלּוֹת וּמַרְכִּין רֹאשׁ, כָּךְ אֲנִי כְּשֶׁנּוֹפֵל עָלַי זֶרֶם הַמַּיִם הַמְרֻפָּשִׁים בְּעֵת עָמְדַתֵךְ הַשַּׁאֲנַנָּה בְּמִקְלַחַת. לִפְעָמִים גַּם יַגִּיעַ אֵלַי קוֹלֵךְ, עָמוּם. אַךְ זֶה רַק לְעִתִּים רְחוֹקוֹת. בְּדֶרֶךְ כְּלָל, רַק שְׁאוֹן הַמַּיִם. עִם הַזְּמָן, זְמָן לֹא רַב כְּלָל, אֶשֶּׂא פָנַי לְמַעְלָה, אֶשֶּׂה פָנַי לְמַעְלָה, פּוֹעֵר פִּי לִקְרַאת מֵימַיִךְ. עוֹד אֵינֶנִּי יוֹדֵעַ אֵיזֶה אִישׁ מְאֹהָב אֲנִי! בְּסַעֲרַת נֶפֶשׁ שֶׁלֹּא נוֹדְעָה דֻּגְמָתָהּ אֲמַלֵּא אֶת פִּי בַּמַּיִם שֶׁנּוֹגְעוּ בְעוֹרֵךְ, אֶעֲבִירֵם מִצַּד לְצַד תּוֹךְ נְפוּחַ לְחָיַי, אֲשַׂחֵק בָּהֶם בַּלְּשׁוֹן! אַךְ הָעִקָּר הוּא לֹא שָׁם, לֹא שָׁם, לֹא בִּנְפִילַת הַמַּיִם הַצּוֹאִים אֶל תּוֹךְ פִּי, לֹא בְּאֵיךְ אֲנִי מִתְאַחֵד אִתָּךְ, בְּאֵיזוֹ אַהֲבָה וְהִתְמַסְּרוּת; הָעִקָּר הוּא לִפְנֵי-כֵן, בַּצְּפִיָּה הַמּוֹרֶטֶת לְהִכָּנֵסֵךְ לַחֲדַר הָאַמְבַּטְיָה. שָׁעוֹת עַל שָׁעוֹת בְּכָל יוֹם, הוֹפֵךְ לְיֵשׁוּת מַמְתִּינָה, לִצְפִיָּה אַדִּירָה לְרֶסֶס מַיִם מְטֻנָּפִים שֶׁל אִשָּׁה אַחַת עַל פְּנֵי כַּדּוּר הָאָרֶץ – הַאִם יֵשׁ תַּכְלִית נַעֲלָה מִזּוֹ לְחַיֵּי אָדָם? הַאֵין אֲנִי מְמַמֵּשׁ אֶת מַה שֶׁחִתַּרְתִּי אֵלָיו שָׁנִים: לְסַבֵּל תַּחְתַּיִךְ בַּחֲשַׁךְ מִבְּלִי שֶׁתֵּדְעִי!"

צְפִיַּת הָאוֹהֵב, שִׂכְחַת הָאֲהוּבָה, וְהַכֹּל עַל רֶקַע מְרֻפָּשׁ – חַיִּים נִכְסָפִים! לֹא אֶזְכֶּה בָּהֶם!

Sternly condemned to eternal imprisonment in a cell, and all this just because I died. And after all I did nobody any harm, *au contraire*, I got weaker and weaker until I fossilized one night into an object. For that you lead me in public, a congregation of gaolers and witnesses and watchers, you among them, to be imprisoned in this cell in the ground. You'll go out of here, but not me. Without a voice I whisper to you, while still on the black trolley on the way to the hole.

"You realise, there's no point in pretending, you're leaving me. I'm condemned to a worse fate than the worms that infest your toilet drain. A hidden dream fills up my heart – to stand there in their stead, pinned to the pipes, I'm not allowed to move, all my life is the expectation of water, your water, falling in the pipes after you've washed or fulfilled a private function, to know we have not concluded our shared interests on the face of the earth. Smiling pleasantly and lowering my head, so am I when a stream of soiled water falls wide upon me as you stand serene in the shower. Sometimes our voice will also reach me, dimly. But that only at distant intervals. Generally just the din of the water. At first I'll lower my head, droplets of water dripping on my head and face. In time, not much time at all, I'll tilt up my face, gaping my mouth wide for your waters. You still don't know what kind of lover I am! In emotional abandon previously unprecedented I'll fill my mouth with water that touched your skin, I'll pass it from side to side puffing my cheeks, I'll swirl it with my tongue! But the main thing is not there, not there, not in the fall of filthy water in my mouth, not in how I become one with you, with what love and dedication; the main thing is before hand, the hair-plucking anticipation for your entrance into the bathroom. Hour upon hour every day, becoming a waiting being, a tremendous anticipation of a droplet of filthy water from one woman on the face of planet earth – can there be a higher meaning than this to the life of man? Am I not fulfilling what I've striven toward for years: to suffer underneath you in the dark without you knowing!"

The lover's expectation, the beloved's forgetfulness, and all against a tainted backdrop – precious life! I will not have the privilege!

גְּהִירָתֵךְ עַל שְׂפַת הַבּוֹר

תָּבִינִי שֶׁלֹּא אוּכַל לַעֲשׂוֹת דָּבָר. אֲנִי הוּא הַמּוּטָל, הַמְצֻפֶּה, בְּתַחְתִּית הַבּוֹר. וּבָרֶגַע הַקָּצָר שֶׁבֵּין הֲנָחַת גּוּפָתִי בְּעֹמֶק לְבֵין כִּסּוּיָהּ בְּשׁוּרַת הַלְּבֵנִים, כְּשֶׁלֹּא יַחֲצֹץ דָּבָר בֵּינֵינוּ, אָז, אִם תִּתְקָרְבִי אֶל שׁוּלֵי הַבּוֹר, צוֹפָה בִּי מִלְמַעְלָה, יָנוּחַ עָלַי לְרֶגַע צֵל רֹאשֵׁךְ וּכְתֵפַיִךְ. הִנֵּה מַגָּעֵנוּ הָאַחֲרוֹן בָּעוֹלָם.

וְאִם יֹאמְרוּ, "הַצֵּל, הֲרֵי הַצֵּל הוּא כָּל מַה שֶּׁאֵינֵךְ, הוּא כָּל קַרְנֵי הָאוֹר הַנֶּחְסָמוֹת בָּךְ!" אֶעֱנֶה, "אֵין דָּבָר, גַּם זֶה טוֹב, הֲלֹא צִלֵּךְ אֵינוֹ אֵינוּת שֶׁל מִישֶׁהוּ אַחֵר, זוֹ הָאֵינוּת שֶׁלֵּךְ!"

אִם יַחֲלֹף אָז עָנָן וְיַסְתִּיר אֶת הַשֶּׁמֶשׁ, אוֹ אָמוּת בַּחֹרֶף וְלֹא יִהְיוּ צְלָלִים, דַּי לִי שֶׁתְּצַיְצִי בִּי. עִם נוּחַ עָלַי מַבָּטֵךְ, קַרְנֵי אוֹר יִשָּׁבְרוּ מִגּוּפָתִי הָעֲטוּפָה שְׁחֹרִים - אַף הִיא מִין צֵל - וְיִשָּׁאֲבוּ אֶל עֵינַיִךְ.

בִּמְהִירוּת רַעֲנָנָה אֶקְפֹּץ אֶל תּוֹךְ מֹחֵךְ, צָלוּפָח כֵּהֶה, אֶמְצָא בָּךְ מִשְׁכָּן, אֲקַנֵּן בָּךְ, תְּחִלָּה בִּרְעָדָה קְטַנָּה, אַחַר-כָּךְ בְּשֶׁקֶט, צֵל קָטָן וְצָנוּעַ. כָּךְ אֶהְיֶה עַד שֶׁאֶדְהֶה.

אַתְּ תַּעֲשִׂי תְּנוּעוֹת כְּשֶׁתֵּלְכִי מִשָּׁם, אָדָם חַי מִתְנוֹעֵעַ וּמִפְרָקָיו חַיִּים; זִכְרִי אֶת הַשָּׂרוּעַ בִּתְנוּחָה קְפוּאָה. הֲלֹא כָּךְ, לְפָחוֹת, הִמְתַּנְתִּי לָךְ גַּם בְּחַיַּי.

You understand, I won't be able to do a thing. I'll be the one thrown down, the one expectant, at the base of the grave. And in the short moment between my body being laid in the depths and being covered up with a line of paving stones, when nothing intervenes between us, then, if you come close to the hole's lip, viewing me from above, the shadow of your head and shoulders will fall on me a moment, that will be our final contact in this world.

And if they should say, "The shadow, why the shadow is all you're *not*, it's all the rays of light obstructed by you!" I'll reply, "Never mind, that's good too, at least your shadow is not the absence of someone else, it's *your* absence!"

If a cloud should pass by then and hide the sun, or I should die in winter when there are no shadows, it is enough for me that you should peek at me. When your gaze rests on me, rays of light will break from my corpse wrapped in black – that too is a kind of shadow – and they'll be drawn to your eyes.

With refreshed vigour I'll leap into your mind, a murky eel, find in you a habitation, make a cocoon, first with a little tremor, then quietly, a small modest shade. So I'll be until I fade.

You will make motions as you go from there, a living person moves and their joints alter; remember the one strewn in a frozen posture. Was it not like that I waited for you, at least in the course of my life.

ההשפלה הגדולה

נִפְחַד עַד עָמְקֵי נִשְׁמָתִי, מְחַכֶּה לְמַהֲלוּמָה הָעֲתִידָה לִנְחֹת בְּכָל רֶגַע - בְּאֵלֶּה כְּבָר הִכַּרְתָּ אוֹתִי עוֹד בְּחַיַּי.

לֹא הִשְׁתַּנֵּיתִי. כַּמָּה עָגוּם שֶׁאֵינֶנִּי יָכוֹל לִסְמֹךְ עַל בִּכְיְךָ! זֶה בָּא לְשָׁרֵת בְּעִקַּר אוֹתְךָ, לָתֵת פֻּרְקָן, וְאַחֲרָיו תִּהְיֶה אֶצְלְךָ הַטַּהֲרוּת; וְאֶצְלִי לֹא תִהְיֶה שׁוּם הַטַּהֲרוּת, אַדְרַבָּא, הִתְלַכְלְכוּת, קְרִישָׁה, חַלְּשָׁה שֶׁאֵין לְשַׁעֲרָה. הַמָּוֶת הוּא מָוֶת אַךְ וְרַק בְּיַחַס לִירֵכַיִךְ, לִצְחוֹקֵךְ, לְהַשְׁתַּנְּתֵּךְ.

וְגַם אִם אֲנִי יוֹדֵעַ עָמֹק בְּלִבִּי שֶׁלֹּא כָּךְ הָעוֹלָם בָּנוּי, בְּכָל זֹאת, עָמֹק עוֹד יוֹתֵר בְּתוֹכִי אֲנִי יוֹדֵעַ: בְּדִיּוּק כָּךְ הָעוֹלָם בָּנוּי!

עַכְשָׁו אַתְּ מַעֲמִידָה פְּנֵי נֶעֱלֶבֶת, מִשְׁתַּמֶּשֶׁת בְּמַה שֶׁאָמַרְתִּי כַּאֲמַתְלָה לִנְטֹשׁ אוֹתִי מַהֵר מִכְּפִי שֶׁתִּכְנַנְתְּ, וְלִי כְּבָר אֵין כֹּחַ לְהַפְצִיר בָּךְ: "חַכִּי! לֹא הֵבַנְתְּ אוֹתִי!"

כִּי הִנֵּה הֵבַנְתְּ אוֹתִי כִּרְצוֹנֵךְ, וּמֵעַתָּה תַּעֲשִׂי כִּרְצוֹנֵךְ, וְאִם תִּרְצִי תֵּלְכִי לְכָאן, וְאִם תִּרְצִי - לְשָׁם. כַּמָּה יָפֶה הוּא רֶגַע הַהַחְלָטָה שֶׁבּוֹ אַתְּ מַחְלִיטָה לִפְסֹעַ לְצַד זֶה אוֹ אַחֵר, הָרֶגַע הַנִּפְלָא וְהַמָּתוֹק הַזֶּה שֶׁל הַחַיִּים שֶׁבּוֹ הָרֶגֶל מַחְלִיטָה לָנוּעַ, וְהִיא אָמְנָם נָעָה, נָעָה לָהּ מִתַּחַת לַשִּׂמְלָה הַמִּתְנַפְנֶפֶת-מִתְרַחֶקֶת.

Scared to the depths of my soul, waiting for the blow bound to fall any minute – like this you've already known me in the course of my life.

I haven't changed. How bleak that I cannot rely on your tears! It comes to service mostly you, to provide a release, and afterward you'll have catharsis; but for me there will be no catharsis, on the contrary, contamination, congealing, weakness beyond reckoning. Death is death only in relation to your thighs, your laugh, your pissing.

And even if I know deep in my heart that the world isn't built that way, nevertheless, even deeper inside me I know: that's exactly how the world is built!

Now you're putting on an affronted air, using what I said as an excuse to leave me sooner than I planned for, and I no longer have the strength to plead: "Wait! You didn't understand!"

For here you've understood me as you please, and as of now you'll do just as you please, and if you please you'll go here and if you please – there. How beautiful the moment of decision when you decide to pace this way or another, that wonderful and sweet moment of life when the leg decides to stir, and does indeed stir, stirs underneath the dress that waves and wanders away.

בְּשׁוֹכְבֵי דוֹמֵם

בְּשָׁכְבֵי דוֹמֵם, רֹאשִׁי לְמַטָּה מְכֻפּוֹת רַגְלַיִךָ, זוֹ הַצָּרָה, מְבִינָה אַתָּ, אַתָּ מֵעָלַי, זוֹ הַצָּרָה,
זוֹ הַצָּרָה! וְאֵין גְּבוּל לְעֶלְבּוֹן! חָלְשָׁתִי מָחְלֶטֶת! אִמְרוּ אַתֶּם, מָה הֱיִיתֶם אַתֶּם עוֹשִׂים
בִּמְקוֹמִי לוּ הֱיִיתֶם מֵתִים הַשּׁוֹכְבִים קְבוּרִים בָּאֲדָמָה וְנִרְקָבִים? לֹא-כְלוּם! לֹא-כְלוּם
בְּיֶדְכֶם לַעֲשׂוֹת! עָנָן פָּעוּט וּמֵצִיק עַד מְאֹד, עֶלְבּוֹן עַד עִמְקֵי הַנֶּפֶשׁ. אֵין לִי מַעֲמָד, מְבִינִים
אַתֶּם? אֶצְלִי לֹא טוֹב, אֶצְלִי הַנּוֹרָא מִכֹּל, מָוֶת וְשִׁעֲמוּם-מָוֶת.

מִי תִרְצֶה לְהִתְחַתֵּן אִתִּי אֲפִלּוּ רֶגַע אֶחָד לְאַחַר מוֹתִי? - גַּם לֹא זְקֵנָה הוֹדִית. עַל אַחַת
כַּמָּה וְכַמָּה אִשָּׁה כָּמוֹךָ שֶׁדּוֹרֶשֶׁת הַרְבֵּה יוֹתֵר, אִשָּׁה כָּמוֹךָ תַּעֲלֹב עַד עִמְקֵי נִשְׁמָתָהּ אִם
תְּקַבֵּל הַצָּעַת אֲרוּסִין מִמֶּנִּי. אֵינִי מֵעֵז. אֲנִי פּוֹחֵד מִתְּגוּבָתֵךְ. אִם אַרְגִּיז אוֹתָךְ, מִי יוֹדֵעַ מָה
אַתָּ עֲלוּלָה לַעֲשׂוֹת, וְלִי אֵין כֹּחַ לְהִתְנַגֵּד.

אֲבָל הַמַּצָּב גָּרוּעַ מִזֶּה: לֹא עוֹשֶׂה כְלוּם, וּמַקֵּף בַּחֹמֶר הַסָּמִיךְ שֶׁל אִי-עֲשִׂיָּתֵךְ כְּלוּם. מָה
הָיָה לָנוּ הַיּוֹם? אִי-מַשֶּׁהוּ. כָּזֶה מַצָּב הָעִנְיָנִים אֶצְלִי. בְּכָךְ אֲנִי עוֹסֵק, אִם תִּשְׁאֲלוּ.

When I lie still, my head beneath the soles of your feet, that's the trouble, you see, you're above, that's the trouble, that's the whole trouble! And there's no limit to the umbrage! My weakness is absolute! Tell me, what would you do in my place, if you were dead and lying buried in the earth and rotting? No-thing. Not a thing would you be able to do! A small and very troubling matter, insulting to the depths of my soul. I've no standing, do you get that? It's not good for me, it's worse than everything for me, death and being bored-to-death.

Who will want to marry me even a minute after my death? Not even an old Bangladeshi woman. Never mind a woman like you who's so much more demanding, a woman like you will be offended to the depths of her soul if she gets an offer to be engaged to me. I wouldn't dare. I'm afraid of your reaction. If I annoy you, who knows what you're liable to do, and I've no power in opposition.

But the situation is worse than that: doing nothing, and surrounded by the thick substance of your not doing nothing. What did we do today? Not something. That's the state of things with me. That's what I'm dealing with, if you should care to inquire.

הציפייה לבואך

הֲנָאָה מֻחְזֶרֶת אֲנִי מוֹצֵא בְּהַקְשָׁתָה פִּתְאוֹמִית שֶׁל הַגַּב תּוֹךְ שְׁכִיבַת פַּרְקְדָן וַאֲמִירָה לְעַצְמִי: "כָּךְ, בִּדְרִיכוּת זֹאת, בְּאִמּוּץ כָּל הַחוּשִׁים, אֲנִי מְחַכֶּה לָךְ!"

בִּתְחִלַּת הַצִּפִּיָּה, כְּחֹדֶשׁ לִפְנֵי בוֹאֵךְ הַמְּיֻחָל, אֲנִי מָתוּחַ לְלֹא נָשׂוֹא. אֵינֶנִּי יוֹדֵעַ אִם תַּגִּיעַ פַּעַם הַשָּׁעָה, כָּל-כָּךְ רְחוֹקָה הִיא. כְּשֶׁעָתַיִם לִפְנֵי בוֹאֵךְ יוֹרֶדֶת עָלַי שַׁלְוַת-מָה, הַהֶשֵּׂג כִּמְטַחֲוֵי-יָד. אֲבָל בְּהַגִּיעַ חֲמֵשׁ הַדַּקּוֹת הָאַחֲרוֹנוֹת, נִרְאֶה שֶׁאֲנִי נִזְרָק שׁוּב אָחוֹר, שְׁנוֹת אוֹר מַפְרִידוֹת בֵּינֵינוּ; שְׁנִיָּה אַחַר שְׁנִיָּה שֶׁל צִפִּיָּה לְקוֹל טְפִיפַת עֲקֵבַיִךְ - כָּל אֵלֶּה גַּלְקְסִיּוֹת שֶׁעָלַי לַעֲבֹר. בַּעֲבוֹדַת פֶּרֶךְ, תָּשׁוּשׁ וּבְלִי, כְּמִי שֶׁהִתְכּוֹפֵף שָׁנִים עַל מָשׁוֹט בִּסְפִינַת עֲבָדִים, אֲנִי מַגִּיעַ אֶל הַשָּׁעָה הַיְעוּדָה. אֵיזוֹ אוֹדִיסֵיאָה!

אֶת הַיְגִיעָה הָעֲצוּמָה תּוּכְלִי לְאֱמֹד טוֹב יוֹתֵר אִם תִּזְכְּרִי שֶׁהַצִּפִּיָּה הַבָּאָה לְבוֹאֵךְ כְּבָר מַתְחִילָה - וְלָמָּה נֹאמַר מַתְחִילָה, נִמְשֶׁכֶת! - מִתּוֹךְ זוֹ הַקּוֹדֶמֶת.

140

I take peculiar pleasure in a sudden curving of my spine while lying prostrate and saying to myself: "Thus, with considerable readiness, with all senses primed, I am awaiting you!"

At the start of anticipation, about a month before your longed for visit, I am in an unbearable state of tension. I don't know if that hour will ever come, it is so distant. About two hours before you arrive a certain tranquillity descends over me, the object is within hand's reach. But when the last five minutes ensue, it seems like I'm thrown back once more, light years intervene, second after second of anticipation of the sound of your rapping heels – all these galaxies I must traverse. Through back breaking labour, worn and threadbare, like someone bent years long over a galley slave's oar, I reach the appointed hour, what an odyssey!

You'll be able to comprehend the huge weariness better if you remember that the anticipation of your coming has already started – and why shall we say started, rather has continued! – since the one preceding.

העבודה

כְּרֶגַע הַמַּצָּב בִּיש. אֲנִי יַגֵּעַ עַד מְוֶת לְאַחַר לַיְלָה שֶׁל צְפִיָּה. מִסְתַּבֵּר שֶׁהַקָּרֵב עָלַיִךְ עוֹד לֹא הֻכְרַע. לֹא חָדְלוּ מִסָּבִיב הַשָּׁאוֹן וְהָאָבָק, עוֹבְדִים לְלֹא לֵאוּת עֲבוֹדַת פֶּרֶךְ: רוֹצִים בָּךְ. כֹּחוֹת אַדִּירִים מִתְגּוֹשְׁשִׁים עַל לִבֵּךְ. חוֹצְבִים, מַכִּים, מְסַתְּתִים לְלֹא הֲפוּגָה. לְאִישׁ כְּבָר אֵין כֹּחַ, מֶחֱלְקָם כְּבָר נִשְׁכְּחָה הַמַּטָּרָה, אֲבָל הַפַּטִּישִׁים עוֹלִים וְיוֹרְדִים.

כֹּחִי אָזַל. אֲנָשִׁים רַעֲנַנִּים בָּאוּ לִשְׁלֹט בָּעוֹלָם. הִנֵּה אַרְכִּין מְעַט אֶת רֹאשִׁי לְמַטָּה וְהַצִּדָּה, וַאֲפַנֶּה אֶת הַדֶּרֶךְ בִּתְנוּעָה חֲצִי-גַּנְדְּרָנִית, גֶ'סְטָה שֶׁאֲנִי עוֹשֶׂה בְּחִיּוּךְ-עֶלְבּוֹן מְעֻקָּם, עִם תְּנוּעַת הַבְּלִיעָה שֶׁל פַּקֶּת הַגַּרְגֶּרֶת.

"אֲבָל שִׁמְעִי", אֲנִי תוֹפֵס בְּשַׁרְווּלֵךְ לְפֶתַע כְּשֶׁאַתְּ עוֹמֶדֶת לַחֲלֹף עַל פָּנַי, "הֲרֵי לֹא בֶּאֱמֶת חָשַׁבְתְּ שֶׁאַרְפֶּה! אֵיךְ אַרְפֶּה? עֲבוֹדָה יוֹתֵר קָשָׁה הִיא סְתִימַת הַגּוֹלֵל עַל אַהֲבָתִי מֵאֲשֶׁר חֲצִיבָתָהּ! אֲנִי כָּאן, לְיָדֵךְ, סְבִיבֵךְ, אַמְצָא לִי מִשְׂרַת מַשְׁגִּיחַ עַל חֲצִיבַת הַמִּנְהָרָה אֵלַיִךְ, בְּעֶרְמוּמִיּוּת רַבָּה אֶפָּטֵר מִן הָעֲבוֹדָה הַגּוּפָנִית הַמְפָרֶכֶת, אֶהְיֶה הַמְמֻנֶּה עַל הַפּוֹעֲלִים הָרַבִּים, וּכְשֶׁנַּגִּיעַ סוֹף סוֹף אֵלַיִךְ, אָז אֲפַשֵּׁט אֶת מַדֵּי הַמַּשְׁגִּיחַ, וְאֶטְמַע בֵּינֵיהֶם וְאֶפְשֹׁט גַּם אֲנִי אֶת יָדִי לַשָּׂכָר!"

"מֵיהוּ הַמְדַלְדֵּל הַנִּדְחָק בֵּינֵיכֶם בְּקוֹל צְוָחָה דַּק?" אַתְּ מוֹרָה בְּאֶצְבַּע לְעֶבְרִי. עַל בְּהוֹנוֹת, בְּרֹאשׁ מֻרְכָּן, אֲנִי נִגָּשׁ וְלוֹחֵשׁ בְּאָזְנֵךְ:

"אֲהוּבָתִי, אֵינֵךְ מַכִּירָה אֶת כֹּחוֹתַי, דַּלִּים מִשֶּׁחָשַׁבְתְּ. בִּשְׁאֵרִית הָאֶנֶרְגְיָה שֶׁלִּי אֲנִי מִתְלַקֵּחַ לִכְבוֹדֵךְ, מֵפִיק אֵשׁ חֲוֶרֶת, כִּמְעַט שְׁקוּפָה, קְצַת אֲוִיר רוֹעֵד מֵעַל לִפְתִיל מְפַיֵּחַ. רְאִי כַּמָּה אֵין בִּי, וְכַמָּה מִתּוֹךְ זֶה אֲנִי מַשְׁקִיעַ לִכְבוֹדֵךְ. כָּל שֶׁתִּתְאַמְּצִי לִרְאוֹת אוֹתִי, כָּל שֶׁתִּתְקָרְבִי אָזְנֵךְ לְהַאֲזִין לְחַלְשַׁת לִבִּי, אָחוּשׁ מִקָּרוֹב אֶת הֶבֶל נְשִׁימָתֵךְ. אַתְּ עַצְמֵךְ לֹא תֵּדְעִי

Right now the situation is dire. I'm dead tired after a night of expectation. Turns out the battle over you isn't over. The din and dust have not let up around me, they're working without cease, slave labour: they're after you. Tremendous forces are wrestling over your heart. Carving, beating, chiselling without let up. No one has any strength left, some have already forgotten the point, but the hammers keep rising and falling.

My strength has waned. Fresh talent has arrived to rule the world. I'll lower my head a little down and to one side, and make way in a semi-flamboyant fashion, a gesture I'll make with a crooked smile, a motion of swallowing my Adam's apple.

"Listen up," I catch your sleeve suddenly when you've almost gone past, "You didn't really think I'd let you go! How can I let go? It's harder work to put the final touches to my love than it was to carve it at all! I'm here, right by your side, all around, I'll find a job overseeing a tunnel to you, with considerable guile I'll shirk the back breaking physical toil, I'll be the supervisor of many labourers, and when we finally reach you I'll strip off my supervisor's cap and lose myself among them and put my hand out for a compensation!

"Who's the wastrel squeezing among you with a feeble warble?" you wag a finger toward me. On tippy toe with my head hung low, I go up and whisper in your ear:

"My love, you do not know my powers, they're poorer than you reckoned. With the last of my strength I'm going up in flames curiously in your honour, putting off a pale fire, almost translucent, a little trembling air above a charcoal wick. See how much there isn't in me and how much of that I'm putting into your honour. The more you strain to see me, the more you put your ear close to my weakened heart, the closer I'll feel up close the vapour of your mouth. You yourself

אֵיךְ הִתְקָרַבְתָּ, אֵיךְ רָכַן רֹאשֵׁךְ עַל חָזִי מִתּוֹךְ סַקְרָנוּת, וְשָׁם נִשְׁאַרְתָּ, וּלְפֶתַע נִהְיֵית שֶׁלִּי,
בִּגְהִירָה זוֹ, אַתְּ וּשְׂעָרֵךְ מְדַגְדֵּג אֶת פָּנַי".

וְאוּלַי בִּכְלָל לֹא תַבְחִינִי בִּי. בַּהֲמֻלָּה הַזֹּאת, בַּקֶּרֶב הַנִּטָּשׁ עָלַיִךְ – מְעַט סִכּוּי יֵשׁ לְחָלְשׁוֹת
וְלִדְמָמוֹת. אֲבָל יוֹם אֶחָד, כְּשֶׁתָּקוּצִי בָּרַעַשׁ, אוֹפִיעַ לָךְ כְּאֶפְשָׁרוּת שֶׁהָיְתָה; שׁוּם דָּבָר לֹא
יָמַּשׁ, מִין לֹא-כְלוּם כָּפוּל: גַּם אֶפְשָׁרוּת, גַּם בְּעֶצֶב. זֶה יִהְיֶה זֶה נִצְחוֹנִי: הָאֲחֵרִים יִתְקְעוּ יָתֵד;
אֲנִי אַקִּיף אוֹתָךְ כְּמוֹ אֲוִיר, תּוּכְלִי לִדְאוֹת, אַרְאֶה לָךְ דָּבָר שָׁקוּף אוֹ שְׁנַיִם, בֵּינֵיהֶם אֲהַבְתִּי.

144

won't know how close you crept, how your head lowered over my breast, and there you stayed, and suddenly you were mine, with that crouch, you and your hair were tickling my face."

But maybe you won't even notice me. In this hubbub, in the battle being waged over you – scant chance for weaknesses and silence. But one day, when you start in the turbulence, I'll appear to you as a possibility that once existed; nothing will be fulfilled, a kind of double nothingness; both possibility and past. That will be my victory: others will sink a post in the ground. I will surround you like the air, you could hang-glide, I'll show you a transparent thing or two, among them my love.

HANOCH LEVIN (1943–1999) was born in Palestine to Holocaust survivors from Poland. Originally a poet, he exploded onto the Israeli theatre scene in 1968 with his play You, Me and the Next War, a sharp critique of the 1967 Six-Day War. The play was extremely controversial and the run ended when some of the actors refused to play their parts. Levin continued to make a name for himself by writing and directing plays that critiqued Israeli society. When his denunciation of the Golda Meir administration, The Queen of the Bathtub, opened in 1970, demonstrations again led to a premature closing. As a consequence, Levin withdrew from the public eye, although he continued writing (56 plays in total, 34 of which were produced), directing many of these plays himself. He continued working until the very end, holding auditions for his newest play from his hospital bed.

ATAR HADARI was born in Israel, raised in England, trained as an actor and writer at the University of East Anglia before winning a scholarship to study poetry and playwriting with Derek Walcott at Boston University. His plays have won awards from the BBC, Arts Council of England, National Foundation of Jewish Culture (New York), European Association of Jewish Culture (Brussels) and the Royal Shakespeare Company, where he was Young Writer in Residence, and have been staged at theatres on both sides of the Atlantic. His Songs from Bialik: Selected Poems of H. N. Bialik (Syracuse University Press) was a finalist for the American Literary Translators' Association Award and his poems have won a number of prestigious literary awards and prizes.

IGAL SARNA was born in Tel Aviv, Israel, in 1952. After serving as a tank commander in the Yom Kippur War in 1973, he was one of the ex-soldiers who founded the Peace Now movement. He received the IBM Tolerance Prize for a series of cover stories he wrote on Iranian political prisoners in Israel, and in 1998 he was awarded a Fulbright grant and spent a semester at the University of Iowa International Writing Program. His books include fiction and nonfiction. He has published, in Hebrew, a biography of the poet Yona Wallach; a novel, *Tzayad Ha-Zikaron* (Hunter of Memory); and most recently, *Muzungu: The Story of the Aeroplane that Crashed on the Moon-Mountains*. A collection of his essays was published in English as *Broken Promises: Israeli Lives* (UK, Atlantic Books), and as *The Man Who Fell Into a Puddle* (US, Pantheon / Vintage). His books have been praised by, among others, *The Times Literary Supplement*: "Sarna touches on all the themes of Israel's modern tragedy. Thoughtful and humane... A marvellous book." He writes feature stories for the daily newspaper *Yediot Aharonot* and lives in Tel Aviv with his wife and two children.